TEAMWORK II

A Dog Training Manual for
People with Physical Disabilities

Revised and Expanded

by Stewart Nordensson and Lydia Kelley

For information address TOP DOG Publications, a 501 (c) (3)
nonprofit organization, 350 S. Williams Blvd., Suite 150, Tucson, AZ.

The proceeds from the sale of this book will aid TOP DOG in its
mission to teach people with physical disabilities to train their own
service dogs.

The ISBN 0-9840553-1-2

Printed in the United States of America

1 2 3 4 5 6 7 8 9 10

Lovingly dedicated...

in memory of all the dogs
who have shared our lives
as helpmates and friends

and in anticipation of
all the helpmates and friends
yet to come

PHOTOGRAPHS
(all photos are listed from top to bottom)

Front Cover

- Samir Madden (bilateral above elbow, bilateral below knee amputee) and Ashka (golden retriever)

- Morris Ardle (osteoarthritis, coronary artery disease) and Cheyenne (lab/chow)

- Tim Morin (spina bifida, scoliosis) and Hinzi (yellow lab)

- Sandra Schwartz (arthritis) and Chance (bouvier des Flanders), Harold Schwartz (arthritis) and Precious (bouvier des Flanders)

- Jane Cords (spinal cord injury T-6) and Zio (labradoodle)

Back Cover

- Jimmy Armijo (cerebral palsy) and Anna (yellow lab)

- Elaine Smith (degenerative arthritis) and Cheeko (lab mix)

- Diane Manchester (multiple sclerosis) and Mojo (labradoodle)

- Robert Ruskin (Parkinson's disease, epilepsy) and Calypso (Belgian sheepdog)

- Bob Alan (osteoporosis, heart transplant) and Oinker (dalmatian/beagle/terrier mix)

TABLE OF CONTENTS

FOREWORD TO FIRST EDITION

We always planned for TEAMWORK to be a two-book series. We knew right from the start that there was simply too much information to fit in one. Originally we planned to write book two in much the same way as book one—with lengthy descriptions of how to teach each exercise. We realized early on, however, that the service exercises are much more individual than the basic obedience skills. So we changed the format and personalized Teamwork II.

We wrote each chapter and then, as much as possible, gave the section or sections to the person written about and asked him or her to read and review them. In each case, valuable information came back. They remembered training tips we'd forgotten or helpful tricks they had tried. We received excellent feedback that helped make this a much stronger book. Best of all we realized once again that this type of training really works. Because they had learned to do the training themselves, they were able to share with us these personal triumphs and adversities, so that we can now share them with you.

Over 50* teams have been certified through the TOP DOG training program to date and many more have benefited from the training although they did not make it all the way to certification. These are the people we turned to to help us make Teamwork II a success. We know that all over the country, indeed all over the world, there are people who have the desire to train their own dogs to help them, lacking perhaps only the know-how. Now you have the knowledge in your hand. Good luck. Enjoy the journey.

*At the publication of this edition, 107 TOP DOG teams have been certified!

ABOUT THE AUTHORS

Stewart Nordensson

Lydia Kelley

Stewart Nordensson was born in Los Angeles, California. He moved to Tucson in 1949. He was born with cerebral palsy and despite severe physical limitations, he began training dogs at about four years of age. Most trainers told him to his face that he couldn't do it himself, which made him all the more determined. He was one of the first people in a wheelchair to take a dog all the way through to a UD (the highest degree in obedience), and he certified four dogs as service dogs.

Stewart was married for 25 years to Donna Veith. Donna suffered from juvenile rhematoid arthritis and was a great help and support to Stewart in his dog training efforts. Donna died in 1991. Stewart carried on, training his own dogs and writing the Teamwork books to help others learn how to train their dogs no matter their physical limitations. Stewart died on October 5, 1999, about a year after Teamwork II was originally published.

Lydia Kelley was born in Albany, NY. She never had a dog growing up, although she always wanted one. When she moved to Tucson in 1970, one of the first things she got was her first dog, a border collie mix, who lived to be 18 ½. Currently, Lydia has two wonderful mixed breed dogs in her life: Shasta, a seven year old chow mix, and Cisco, a six year old doberman mix. They love their home in the desert, and also enjoy traveling regularly together in a small motorhome, especially enjoying national parks and forests throughout the U.S. and Canada.

INTRODUCTION TO THE REVISED AND
EXPANDED EDITION

When Stewart and I finished Teamwork II eleven years ago, we knew it wasn't the end, only the beginning. The beginning of reaching out across the country, even around the world to help people with disabilities learn to train their own dogs to be helpmates. There's so much that dogs can learn to do for their owners. All people needed was the know-how. That's what the Teamwork books provide.

Stewart died in 1999. As I worked on this revision, I missed his invaluable input; I missed his wisdom and understanding; and I missed his wonderful (sometimes kooky) sense of humor. He knew so much about dogs and how to work with them. He was the inspiration for the founding of TOP DOG, and his memory continues to inspire those of us who knew him. His legacy carries on in these books and videos, helping and inspiring people with disabilities all around the world.

TOP DOG continues to go strong, training people with many different physical disabilities to train their dogs to become more than just companions, to become extensions of themselves. We continue to learn as much as we teach, and all this new knowledge is reflected in this expanded and updated version of Teamwork II.

In the original forward, we explained that Teamwork II had to be written a little differently than Teamwork. We realized that the service exercises are much more individual than the basic obedience skills. So we changed the format and personalized Teamwork II. We wrote each chapter from a specific person's point of view, with our additions of hints, cautions, and reminders. Using people's own experiences showed us once again that this type of training really works. Because they had learned to do the training themselves, they were able to share with us their experiences, so that we could share them with you.

In this edition, we have added a chapter with a couple of new helpful exercises to teach your dog, and we changed the order of some chapters. We believe this is a better way of progressing through the skills necessary to assist your dog in becoming a service dog. But you'll find that our basic philosophy of dog training remains the same. If you look at your dog as a living, breathing, thinking creature with a huge capacity to love and offer help, then this book and the experiences of these people will help you teach him all the skills you need. Your life will be made easier, and it will be brighter and richer from sharing it with your dog. You will have TEAMWORK!

Lydia Kelley
May 2010

Chapter 1

GETTING STARTED
How to Use this Book Effectively

Ilene had trained her border collie, Noah, by herself. Noah performed many service exercises as well as alerting Ilene to sounds that she was unable to hear. But most important was the bond formed by living and working together. Ilene believed strongly that because she had trained Noah herself they understood one another and were a better team than if someone had trained the dog for her. She really saw Noah's perception when Ilene began a new job in a courtroom in Maryland. She took Noah to meet all their new co-workers and he greeted each politely, but without excitement. When the judge came in, however, Noah went directly to him and bowed deeply with great respect. Ilene referred to Noah as "my little brown-noser."

This book will help you learn how to train your dog to the level of service dog — a dog who is well-behaved, well-trained and well-socialized, a dog who can accompany you to places like the mall. The author Stewart Nordensson with his yellow lab, Laura

Getting help from a friend is like using any other training tool. Here, Nancy's husband, George, hands her a treat while Nancy praises her dog for the sit. Nancy Mairs (multiple sclerosis) and Pupkin (yellow lab)

This training manual is designed for people with disabilities to learn how to train their own dogs to be service dogs. It is intended as a companion manual to Teamwork. If you have not read Teamwork, you can still use this book, but you will be at a disadvantage. Space will not permit us to repeat all the philosophy that is contained in Teamwork, nor can we repeat all the basic obedience training. But it's critical that you have both a good teaching philosophy and a solid foundation of basic obedience before you attempt the more complex exercises contained in this book. We highly recommend that you read Teamwork, so that both you and your dog are ready for Teamwork II.

If you are one who learns better visually, we recommend that you use the Teamwork videos (available in VHS and DVD) in conjunction with this manual. The videos demonstrate each exercise, so that you can watch how it's done. We also have Teamwork on audio CD, and Teamwork II will soon be on CD as well.

Our books are written with the understanding that because you have some sort of physical disability, you must approach training in a different way. It doesn't mean you can't do the training yourself; it just means traditional methods may not work for you. All previous training books have assumed that the trainer has certain physical abilities, that walking, talking, and making corrections are not problems. Because Stewart, one of the authors of this book, had cerebral palsy and found that walking, talking, and making corrections were quite difficult, he spent years devising alternative training methods. These methods don't just work for him. They have been proven to work for many individuals with various disabilities.

DISABILITIES

As stated, Stewart had cerebral palsy. How it affected him is different from how others are affected by CP, and it is different from how someone is affected by arthritis, a spinal cord injury, or multiple sclerosis. In other words, disabilities vary greatly, and people with the same disability vary greatly. So there is not one right way for a disabled person to train a dog.

If you're reading this book, it's assumed that you have a dog that you believe can help you in your day-to-day life. What you need your dog to do will differ from what the next person wants from his or her dog, even if that person has the same disability. We suggest ways to teach each exercise, taking into account your needs and abilities. Only you can decide which exercises will be a help to you and which ones to skip. As you become accomplished in teaching your dog these skills, you will gain the expertise to perhaps teach him something we haven't even thought of. This is the advantage of doing the training yourself. You know best what help you need from your dog.

Be aware of your health when teaching any skill. If you are tired, irritable, weak, or in intense pain, wait until you are feeling better. Your dog will recognize your discomfort, but he may not know how to respond. You need to be positive, calm, and alert to stay on top of your training sessions so that he can learn and build on success.

DOGS

Dogs are as individual as people. If you found your dog intelligent and eager to learn during basic obedience lessons, you still need to consider some factors before trying to train him to be a service dog. Willingness is an important consideration, but you must also think about what you'll be asking him to do. Some of the tasks you might ask him to perform include picking up large objects, pulling or pushing your wheelchair, bracing to help you up or down, and opening doors. These exercises all require a medium-to-large, fairly strong dog. It would be difficult for a chihuahua or a miniature poodle to help you up or pick up heavy items for you.

Your dog should be young enough to be able to accept new and distracting situations. An older dog becomes quite set in his ways and doesn't like his routine disturbed. On the other hand, a puppy can't handle too much stimulation and may react by becoming afraid. Under eight months of age, your dog shouldn't do more than go to a puppy kindergarten class with lots of socialization. If he is over five years you may have trouble teaching him all you want him to learn, and he may be overwhelmed by too many changes in his life.

Temperament is a very important factor. If your dog is too shy or too aggressive to handle public exposure, don't take him out in public. Be content to teach him to help you at home.

As in Teamwork we use the male gender in referring to your dog throughout this book. That does not imply a preference for male dogs. Both sexes are equally trainable. A neutered dog, either male or female, is much easier to work with, less distracted, calmer, neater. But our use of "he" is for simplification only.

TRAINING TOOLS

In Teamwork, we stressed the importance of doing as much of the work as possible for yourself. That's the whole point of using a training manual, and you will find that you can do much more than you thought possible if you follow our methods.

There might be times when you will need the help of a friend to get through certain exercises. If you do it correctly, you will still be doing the training yourself. You will simply be using a person as a training tool.

For instance, if you can't hold a food treat in your hand, a friend can stand very close to you, and when your dog completes the exercise, your friend can put a treat in your hand or your lap. To your dog, the reward has magically appeared and it seems to come from you. You give the command, the praise, and the treat.

You may not be able to put a collar on your dog. (Please see the "Equipment" chapter in Teamwork. We give lots of hints on ways you might be able to do it yourself). But remember that even if someone puts the collar and leash on your dog so that you are able to work with him, you are the one who is training your dog. You will give your dog commands to get into his collar, and you will give the praise and reward. You are in charge.

Be careful that your friend doesn't overstep the bounds. No one else should guide your dog into position, or make leash corrections, or give commands—except in emergency situations. Training must come only from you. If you take the time to follow our methods with patience, you will be able to teach your dog every command you want him to learn.

Don't feel less in command if you have to ask for help along the way. Used properly, a person helping you is as much a training tool as the collar, the halter, and the food reward.

BACK TO BASICS—"SLOW IS FAST"

Just as in Teamwork, you will find those three little words—"slow is fast"—throughout this book, reminding you of one of our most important philosophies of dog training. If you rush your training, you build a sloppy foundation. We hope that you took the time with the basics to build the solid foundation you need now. If your dog is shaky in the basic obedience exercises—sit, down, stay, come, and heel—you may have a very difficult time teaching him the service exercises contained in this book.

Review the basics with your dog now. Does he sit when you give him one verbal command, or do you have to repeat the command several times or use physical correction? Does he go promptly into the down position when you tell him? Does he stay in position when you command him to stay, or only when he feels like it? Does he come to you quickly and directly when you call him? Does he even look at you when you call?

You want your dog to have the basics so deeply ingrained that it is a natural instinct to obey your command—as natural as sniffing and scratching. He doesn't have to think about it; he just does it.

When you work on the service exercises contained in this book, especially when you try to practice them in public places, your dog may get confused. It's a common occurrence. When that happens, go back to basics. Give him some commands he knows well and obeys readily. That will help him succeed and calm both of you.

Take some time now, before you go any further in Teamwork II, to put him through his paces in the basic obedience exercises. Work on anything that isn't truly solid. It will help you immensely in the long run.

PARTS OF AN EXERCISE

When you taught your dog "sit" or "down" it was a single action. You commanded your dog to down, he lay down, you praised him. The exercise was over. "Come" was a little more complex. "Come" had two parts to it—coming to you and sitting near you. Your dog had to complete both parts before he had completed the exercise.

Many of the exercises contained in this manual have several parts to them. A simple retrieval exercise, for example, has at least five parts. Your dog must go and get the object; he must pick up the object; he must hold the object; he must bring the object to you; he must give you the object. In some cases your dog must also learn to sit in a certain place so you're able to grasp the object, or raise his head up to you, or put his front paws on you.

So teaching "take it" is not a matter of giving one command and getting a single response. You must break the exercise down into its component parts and teach each part separately and thoroughly. If you skip a part or jump ahead or move too quickly through a part, your dog will probably become confused when he tries to put the exercise together. Then you will become frustrated and wonder why he's disobeying you. Remember that your dog is not willful or malicious. He doesn't dream up ways to aggravate you. If he's not doing the exercise correctly, it's because you haven't taught it to him in the proper sequence.

Always look at each part of the exercise. First, think about what he's doing wrong; then go back one or two steps until you find the place where he's confused. Start at the beginning and work through all the steps again. Remember that slow is fast.

COMMANDS

In teaching most basic obedience exercises, you learned to give your dog the command in a firm, crisp, and quiet tone of voice. You were able to convey that this was something you expected him to obey without having to raise your voice. Only the come command was issued in a high, happy

Practice basic obedience thoroughly both at home and in public until you and your dog are a smooth-working team. Know that he will promptly obey every command no matter the distractions. Top—Jimmy Armijo (cerebral palsy) and Anna (yellow lab)
Bottom—Tim Morin (spina bifida, scoliosis) and Hinzi (yellow lab)

tone of voice, teaching him that coming to you was always a positive experience. He learned to obey the come command, just as he learned to obey sit and down.

You will find as you read this book that most of the service exercises are taught using a high, happy tone during the teaching phase. Your dog will still learn that there is a word associated with an action, but because these exercises are more complex, they must be taught in an upbeat, deliberate manner. Once he learns all the aspects of retrieving an object, for instance, you can command "take it," in a firm crisp tone. He will understand all the steps involved and will go out, get the object and bring it back to you. He will need lots of reassurance and encouragement in order to learn all the steps. As long as you remember to use the same word to mean the same thing every time, your dog will come to understand it as a command.

SIGNALS

As we wrote in Teamwork, we understand that many people are unable to issue verbal commands. You will devise your own system of signals that you and your dog understand. Dogs are great students of body language—it's how they communicate, and they watch our movements much more closely than we think. Therefore, it's not difficult to teach a dog using signals. You just have to be as consistent as you can be, so that the same signal means the same thing each time. No one else may be able to understand, but your dog will know. And that's all that matters.

If you have good hand and arm movement, you can use fairly broad signals at first, exaggerating each movement so your dog can easily see it. As he learns the command, you can make the movements smaller so he will learn to pay even closer attention to you. Remember to be consistent—one signal for each command. Even if you have a lot of involuntary movement, you can still approximate the same movement every time for each command. Despite extra motion, your dog will come to recognize the signal.

If you have trouble moving your hands and arms, you can use your legs and feet as signals. In teaching basic obedience, you must already have worked out a good communication system with your dog. Keep it up. You and your dog will work out the signals that serve your purpose.

Throughout this book, when we tell you to give a command or to praise your dog, it means use words if you can, sounds if you can't make words, and signals if you can't make sounds. It means do whatever you have to do to convey the idea to your dog. And be as consistent as you can to use the same word/sound/signal to mean the same thing every time.

HOW TO USE THIS BOOK

This is not a "do it our way or it won't work" book. There are some basic absolute rules that you should follow, such as: give your dog lots of praise, never hit him, teach rather than correct, take your time in each part of each exercise, work in small increments, and analyze and understand each step before you teach it to your dog. Beyond that, this book provides examples of how certain service exercises were taught by people with various disabilities. They are intended to give you general ideas, stimulate your own creative process, and illustrate some of the difficulties encountered.

In other words, you must begin to work with your dog as a team. We give you the fundamentals; you fill in the blanks.

Through it all, keep your sense of humor. It will be hard work, but you should also find it enjoyable. You can have a good time and still achieve great success. You may encounter frustrations and setbacks along the way but if you keep a positive perspective on what you're trying to accomplish you will succeed. Training a service dog is a big undertaking but the rewards are enormous.

So have fun!

Chapter 2

LEADERSHIP
Learn to Be Top Dog in Your Pack

Leadership is something that is earned over time spent working and living with your dog. It's not something that's automatic. Until we learn a lot more about dogs and how they think, we tend to perceive them as we perceive each other and try to deal with them in that way. On an application to TOP DOG a prospective student answered the question "what do you do when your dog misbehaves," with the statement: "I explain to him why chewing on the plants is not good for him.... So far it hasn't helped." What a surprise!

A leader is one who is in charge or in command—the influential voice. Most of us don't think of ourselves as leadership material, but in our interaction with our dogs we must redefine our role. Humans and dogs do not view the world in the same way, so it's important to look at things from your dog's point of view.

PACK RELATIONSHIP

We talked in Teamwork about the fact that dogs are pack animals. Because they are descended from wolves, we can learn much of how dogs think by learning a little about wolves. Within a wolf pack, there is a social structure that is clearly understood by all members. Leaders exercise control over the pack, usually by such subtle means that an outsider would be unable to recognize them. A mere glance from an alpha wolf will cause others in the pack to crouch in submission.

Your dog considers himself a pack member. Even if it's only you and your dog in your household, you are a pack. That means that there has to be a pack leader and that must be you. Since you have taught him basic obedience, hopefully you have attained pack leader status.

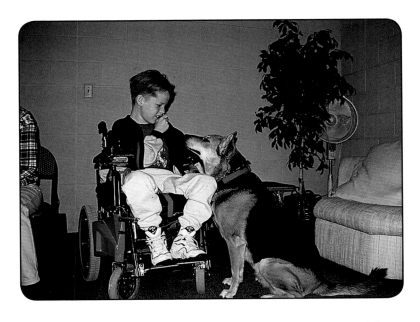

Before you can teach your dog anything new or even practice what he already knows, you must be able to get his attention. It's an important part of your leadership. Mike Rouzaud (muscular dystrophy) and Rosie (shepherd mix)

Understand that this is an ongoing process. Some dogs have dominant personalities, and they will take every opportunity to challenge your authority. These challenges may be subtle, and if you aren't on top of every situation, your dog may slowly wrestle leadership away from you.

Does that mean you have to fight your dog to establish your control? Absolutely not. Remember that the dominant wolf is able to control the pack with a look. If you own a dog with a very dominant personality, one that challenges you often or growls at you as you start to assert yourself, please consult a dog behaviorist in your area. You need to learn how to present yourself to the dog so he can recognize you as the pack leader.

With the vast majority of dogs you will achieve leadership and control simply by your day-to-day interactions. As long as you are fair and consistent in the ways you deal with him, he will be happy to give you the reins of authority.

Here are some simple ways in which you can exercise leadership over your dog in your daily interactions. They use the most basic of his instincts and put you in control of them, serving as constant reminders that you are in charge.

FEEDING

It's very important that you are the one who feeds your dog. We offered suggestions in Teamwork on ways to do the feeding yourself. If you are physically unable to put the food in the bowl and put the bowl on the floor, you must still be present at feeding times. Give your dog commands that show him that you're in charge of his feeding.

Make him sit or lie down while the food is being prepared. Alternate the position you require him to assume so that he isn't just doing it by habit, but he's actually obeying your command. Make him wait in that position, even when his food is put down before him. When you're ready, give him a command to eat. If you're consistent, he will learn quickly whatever he has to do to get his food. It's a great motivator, and it puts you in charge of his most basic of needs.

If you can't handle the bowl yourself, try to devise a way to make it seem as if you are, such as a pail with the handle hanging from your wheelchair or a raised feeding platform. At the very least, you should remain next to his bowl while he eats.

When he's finished, pick up his bowl and put it away. Talk to him while this is going on. Don't leave his bowl down except at feeding times. If he can decide when he wants to eat, you have lost the advantage.

PLAY

You need to be in control of playtime. If you have a dog that loves to fetch the ball, he will constantly bring you a ball and plop it in your lap. If you throw it every time he brings it, he is in charge of play.

You should initiate play sessions. When you feel like it, pick up his ball, get his attention, and throw it. Make sure he brings it back to you; don't chase him for it. You can make chase a totally separate game, but fetch must include your dog bringing the ball all the way back to you. This is important for teaching retrieve exercises later.

If your dog brings you the ball unsolicited, simply put it on the floor and say, "not now," or some similar phrase. You must be strong and resist those pathetically sad eyes that beg you to play. If you can't resist, make him obey two or three commands—sit, down, shake hands. Then you can pick up the ball and act as if playing was your idea.

Any time you feel like playing with your dog, use a command for play. If you use the same word every time, he will come to recognize it as a signal that playing is alright. Because he enjoys the play sessions, he will quickly come to associate the word with the positive tone of voice and the fun results. Stewart taught his dog to play on command, and this made it easier when a new dog came into his household. He gave Laura her play command, immediately putting her into a happy mode and avoiding the possibility of a fight.

Play is an important interaction between you and your dog. Dogs learn a lot through playing. It can also be very good exercise, and most dogs, especially service dogs, don't get enough physical exercise to keep them healthy and happy. Choose the right games—fetch, chase, find—and avoid ones that may stimulate dominant tendencies, such as tug-of-war and rough-housing. Taking your dog for a long walk or even a run (in the cool of the morning or evening), or arranging play-dates with friends' dogs will give him healthy exercise.

Play can also provide time for bonding and training. Kellie taught her German shepherd, Atlee, to "take a lap." This meant to run all the way around the pool. Helen taught her papillon, Flutter, to spin in circles, both to the right and to the left. Betty has her husky mix, Tikaani, walk on the treadmill. Linda works with her lab mix, Jessie, on rally exercises. There are other activities you can share with your dog. Just make sure you stay in control, and keep it fun.

HOUSE RULES

As pack leader you decide the rules of the house and then stick to them. As long as you're consistent in enforcing the rules, your dog will be fine with them. If you don't want your dog underfoot when you're cooking, you can make him stay out of the kitchen. If you don't want him bothering company at the dinner table, you can make him go and lie down while you eat. To make the rules stick, you'll have to be very firm in teaching them. Don't give up when he comes in the kitchen for the twentieth time. Be resolved that you're going to win. He will test you, but he will accept the rule once he sees that you are serious.

You can allow your dog up on the furniture if that's your choice. If you don't want him up, then you must consistently tell him "off." And praise when he's off. If you have a dominant dog that challenges your leadership at every turn, it's probably better if you only allow him up on the sofa on your command. If he comes up on his own, firmly tell him "off." Most dogs will obey. Then after a moment or two, you can invite him to come up. If he refuses to move, and you're unable to pull him off, then you or a friend should tip the sofa over until he has no choice but to get off. This shows him that you mean business.

In all of these dealings, you don't need to be rough or loud with your dog. You have to be firm and patient and determined. Whatever rules you have should be made clear and enforced with consistency by all household members. Then there's no confusion and no chance for a challenge to your authority.

BATHROOM

This may seem strange, but you want to be in charge of your dog's elimination, even after he's well housebroken. This is easiest to teach during housebreaking, but older dogs can learn as well.

Every time you take your dog out to go to the bathroom, use a word or phrase—"potty," "find a spot," "hurry up," whatever you want to use. Your dog was going to eliminate anyway, but it puts you in control of the situation. Use a happy tone of voice because this isn't a command. It's a reminder.

This can be very helpful when you take him places with you. It's always a good idea to make sure he goes to the bathroom before you go into a mall or movie theater. Your dog has come to associate the phrase with the action. So when he hears you say the phrase, it gives him the idea to go. If he doesn't go, it probably means he really doesn't have to.

The pack leader always goes first. Teach your dog to wait at doorways until you give him permission to go through. Jack Stumpenhorst (polio) and Missy (lab mix)

GOING OUTSIDE

The pack leader always goes first. Dogs instinctively know this. So if your dog is always pushing out the door past you, he is the pack leader.

In Teamwork, we taught wait at the door. Please refer to that chapter if you are having trouble at doorways. You must teach him to wait at every door. Then you must give him permission to go outside. It may be that because of your disability, it's necessary for your dog to go ahead of you through doorways. That's okay, as long as he does it on your command.

CONCLUSION

If you observe yourself interacting with your dog, you will see many other places where you can and should maintain control. Think about how he views each situation. If in doubt, give a command. Be consistent in the word or phrase you use. You will see that more and more your dog will come to respect your leadership and look to you for direction and guidance. You are the pack leader; you are in charge.

Chapter 3

EQUIPMENT
A Look at Various Tools to Help You Train Your Dog

About 35 years ago, Stewart learned a valuable lesson about proper equipment. He had a huge German shepherd that he would take for long walks beside his electric scooter. The dog, Joe, was generally well behaved and they enjoyed wandering through all parts of Tucson. One morning as they were exploring a different area of town, Joe suddenly pulled away from Stewart. The cheap leash snapped and Stewart was left holding one end as he watched Joe leap over a wall. Moments later he returned, proudly carrying a chicken in his mouth. Stewart quickly turned around and took Joe and the chicken home. He never went back to that area, and from then on his leashes have always been top of the line.

We went into great detail in Teamwork on various kinds of training and adaptive equipment. Since you have already trained your dog in the basics, we assume you have found the collar and leash that work best for you. So this is just a brief review of training equipment, plus more detail on useful items when you take him out in public.

COLLARS

Your dog should wear some kind of a buckle collar at all times. This should hold his proper county license and other identification should he become lost.

Training collars are for training only. Never leave any kind of a training collar on your dog unattended. The choke collar can be especially danger-ous because it can, in fact, choke him to death. Always remove it when you're not working with him.

You must use the training collar correctly for it to be effective. That is with the "jerk and release." The collar is tight around the dog's neck for no more than a second, and this correction is followed immediately with praise.

An alternative to the traditional training collar is a head halter. Check with your vet for proper fit and use of the halter, and refer to Teamwork for details. It's important that it be used correctly. The head halter may be a wonderful way to go, but if you find you are unable to put the halter on and off, it may not be the best tool for you. If you can put on a training collar but can't work the halter, the collar will be the better training tool simply because you can do it yourself. If you have to get help to put on any training device, then it doesn't matter. Choose the one that works best for you and your dog, and accept help graciously in getting your dog ready to work.

LEASHES

The correct leash is the one that feels best in your hands and does the things you want it to do. If you're unhappy with your current leash, go into any large pet store, or check on line, or in a catalog such as Omaha Vaccine, Dr. Foster and Smith, or R.C. Steele. There are 2-foot, 4-foot, and 6-foot leashes in nylon and leather. There are long lines from ten to fifty feet. There are retractable leashes, combining long and short. There are double loop leashes that you can attach to your wheelchair and still hang onto eas-ily. Check out all the equipment available and find what is best for you.

The head halter can be a very helpful training tool, making it possible for you to control and train your dog yourself. Diane Manchester (multiple sclerosis) and Mojo (labradoodle)

You can carry small items in easy reach in a shoulder pack which will not overload your dog. Blake Gigli (spinal cord injury T 12) and Savannah (golden retriever)

HARNESS

The harness has many uses. It can be a big help for you if you wish your dog to pull you in your manual wheelchair, or if you're ambulatory and you want him to help you up curbs, steps or ramps.

There are different types of harnesses. You want to be sure to get one that's correct for pulling. The best way to get a proper fit is to take your dog with you to the store and get assistance. Try to avoid a harness with too many metal buckles, especially if you're out in the sun with him. If you have trouble with buckles, see if you can find one with Velcro. You might need to adapt it to your needs. Be creative in making it work for you; just be sure it fits your dog correctly so he will use the proper muscles.

Your dog might need some time to get used to wearing a harness, but generally, it doesn't bother a dog at all. If it fits properly, it's just like the buckle collar.

PACKS

Dogs can help their owners by carrying small items in a pack. If you intend to use a pack on your dog, we recommend that you consider a shoulder pack rather than a backpack. Shoulder packs are small so you won't overload your dog, and they put the weight where a dog is best able to handle it. If you have a big bulky backpack, you may be tempted to put too much in it. Your dog will carry whatever you put in without complaint, but in time he may wear down physically and you may shorten his life.

Shoulder packs are worn over the shoulder, and you can put in small items such as keys, money or medications. Those items are then within easy reach but won't overload your dog. You can also grip the pack for balance or for pulling your chair. In fact, many packs come with handles for you to hang onto.

CART

If you routinely have to take a lot of supplies with you, you might want to teach your dog to pull a small cart.

You may need to have one designed specifically for you. It should be made of lightweight material and sit stably on easy rolling wheels. You will have to devise a way to attach the cart to your dog's harness. You can simply use straps on each side of your dog, but the cart may bump into his back legs, especially on the downhill. You can help by holding onto the side of the cart to control speed. A solid tongue will keep the cart a set distance from your dog, but makes it heavier and more awkward to maneuver. The harness should be a proper one for pulling so that he will use the correct muscles.

A cart may be very useful but you may have to design one for your specific needs. Sandra Schwartz (arthritis) and Hoss (bouvier des Flandres)

See chapter 14 "Pull," for ideas on training your dog to pull a cart. Always keep his health in mind. He should have a thorough vet check before you even begin. Tell the vet what you will be requiring of your dog, so he or she can make sure all joints and muscles are sound. If you see any sign of soreness or lameness you should stop having him pull the cart and get him to your vet.

CONCLUSION

Equipment is very important in training and going out with your dog. Whatever collar or leash, pack or cart you decide to use should always be of good quality. If you scrimp on your equipment, you'll be replacing it often. A broken collar or leash is not only inconvenient, but it can be downright dangerous. You want your equipment to last a long time, so be willing to spend a little more to get good quality. It's definitely worth it in the long run.

Chapter 4

IN PUBLIC
Rights, Responsibilities, and Privileges of Owning a Service Dog

Stewart and a friend, Kathy, were eating in a restaurant in Phoenix. They were tired after a long day of seminars on service dogs where Stewart's border collie, Annie, had performed well, showing many skills. Annie went under the table and fell asleep while the humans reviewed the day, including what a great representative Annie was. When they finished their meal, Stewart and Kathy picked up their stuff and headed for the car. At the door they looked at each other and realized they had forgotten something very important...Annie was still sleeping under the table.

We talked at the end of Teamwork about preparing to take your dog out in public. We will repeat the most important points here.

If you have a shy dog, it's critical that you don't overwhelm him. You must build up his confidence very slowly and carefully to help him overcome his fear. This may take months of careful work. You may spend weeks just taking him out of your car in a mall parking lot, then getting right back in and going home. You cannot push the shy dog; the stress will be too much. If he doesn't seem to be getting more secure on these outings, you may need to face the fact that he will probably be too timid to be of service in public. If you push him, the stress will be too much, and he may react aggressively.

If you have an aggressive dog, don't even consider taking him out in public. If a service dog bites someone or reacts aggressively to people or dogs, it will reflect badly on service dogs everywhere. There are many people who do not want dogs around, who are just looking for an excuse to get them banned. Taking a service dog out in public is a great responsibility. Please take this responsibility seriously. If you don't trust your dog out in public, consider keeping him as a pet at home and getting a new dog to train as a service dog. Or perhaps you only need your dog to help you at home. You can still teach your shy or aggressive dog to perform many helpful skills for you in the comfort and safety of your own home.

IN PUBLIC

Most dogs love going with their owners and they can learn to cope with the world as long as you take it slowly. Consider going out in public just another exercise and remember "slow is fast." Don't be surprised if your dog behaves as if he never heard that word "sit" or "down." This is a new environment and he has to learn that the commands mean the same thing no matter where you are. Start at the beginning with each exercise in each new place. Your dog will catch up quickly because he's learned how to learn. But be patient. Use food and lots of praise.

When your dog is obeying each command at home promptly and consistently, go to a quiet park or schoolyard. Work several sessions, running through all the obedience commands. Remember to give appropriate praise and a treat when he does it correctly. With practice, he will become just as solid in public as he is at home. Don't expect perfection the first time out. That's unrealistic and it puts too much pressure on both of you.

Next, go to a shopping center and work your dog in the parking lot. Be very conscious of the temperature of the pavement. Never work on blacktop when it's hot. Your dog's feet are very sensitive.

When he is doing his basic obedience exercises with confidence in these settings, stand with him near the entrance to a busy store. Command him to sit or lie down while people pass by. If people want to pet your dog, you have the right to say yes or no. If your dog is very shy or very friendly, you should say no until you have done this exercise several times. You want this to be a positive experience and you want to maintain control. Don't let strangers crowd around your dog. Tell them he's in training as a service dog and can't be petted. When you feel you have good control, you can allow one person to approach him. Your dog should not back away from or jump up to greet the person. If your dog is calm, you can keep him in a sit or down stay. But it's better to give him permission to greet the person. Tell him "say hi," or "visit" or some phrase that will mean he can approach the stranger and be petted. Correct with "uh-uh-uh" if your dog gets too excited, and ask the person to move away until you regain control. This may take weeks or months to accomplish. Do it slowly and positively and you'll be rewarded for your patience.

Your first trip into the mall should be early on a weekday. Talk to your dog in a happy manner as you approach automatic doors. If the doors startle him, move away and keep talking to him. Remember not to say "it's okay," so you don't reinforce incorrect behavior. Step back and watch others coming and going. Then come up to the doors again talking to your dog in a happy voice. Build up his confidence in a gradual, positive manner.

Sound reverberates inside a mall. Your dog's hearing is much better than yours, so think how all of that noise assaults his ears. Be patient and understanding. He may not hear you as well with all the distractions, so be sure to get his attention before you give a command. He may become confused and disoriented. That's why you want to go back to basics each time you go to a new place. Use your food reward just as you did when you began teaching sit and down.

Once he understands that your commands still mean the same thing, even in this strange environment, he will quickly obey. Then you can take him to the mall during a more crowded time and work on the basics again.

The mall is just one example of a crowded place you might take your dog. You must evaluate all the places in your life where you need him to accompany you. Look at your workplace, school rooms and theaters from his point of view. What obstacles and distractions have you never noticed before? What commands do you have to teach before you ever go out? Commands like reverse and under are invaluable. (See the appropriate chapters.) If you're in a wheelchair you may need to teach him to go behind your chair when you enter doorways or in narrow aisles. Start now and be consistent.

We have included some of the common situations you may face when taking your dog with you. This is by no means every circumstance, but it will give you some ideas on various situations, what to look for, and how to handle them.

RESTAURANTS

More and more people with disabilities are taking their dogs with them to restaurants. It's good for your dog to be with you, it's good for you to have him there, and it's good for the public to see a well-behaved dog in such a setting. So be sure your dog is well-behaved before you ever take him to a restaurant.

Your dog should never eat food off the floor or, worse, off of a plate in a public restaurant. If he has a tendency to clean crumbs from the floor, work very hard to teach him that this is unacceptable. Work on the leave-it command at home until you have confidence that he will obey.

If you never feed your dog from the table, he will never expect it, but you will still have to watch when you're in a restaurant. Some well-meaning waitress may offer him scraps or a steak bone. Politely, but firmly, refuse. Explain the importance of your dog not eating food off the floor or taking it from strangers. Say he's on a strict diet, that strange foods make him sick.

You may also have to ask people not to pet your dog. If too many come up and bother you, just say he's in training and it would be better if they didn't pet him.

You must teach your dog to go under the table and get out of the way. (See chapter 6—Under.) It's an important exercise to teach if you frequent restaurants. Practice with different kinds of tables and booths. If you have a big dog and a small table, have him lie beside you. Make sure his feet and tail are out of the way. You might work on a "tuck your tail" command. (See appendix.) If he shifts positions and stretches out, get him up and reposition him correctly.

Take him to restaurants at off-times at first. Don't go into a crowded noisy place until you both have confidence. If you go to a buffet, you will have to choose between taking your dog through the line with you or leaving him on a stay at the table. Taking him is awkward as you put food on your plate while watching him, and leaving him is potentially dangerous. Have a friend stay at the table and keep an eye on him the first few times you try this. In fact, it's always safest if someone is at the table with your dog.

When you have completed your meal and are ready to leave the table, there's an important thing to remember: your dog. A well-trained and ex-

You must practice many skills before your dog will lie quietly in a restaurant. He must know "under," "down," "stay" and "leave it." Here, friends Mary George and Blake Gigli have lunch while their golden retrievers Sedona and Savannah relax under the table. They are celebrating Savannah's seventh birthday.

perienced service dog will go under the table and sleep. The best thing that you can hear as you leave a restaurant is: "I didn't even know there was a dog here."

When your dog gets up, tell him not to shake. If he's wearing a pack or a harness, adjust it for him and keep a hand lightly on his back until you're sure he won't shake. It's a common thing for a dog to do when he gets up, but if he shakes a clump of hair into the soup at the next table, you will not have made a good impression.

You may find that some restaurants are not suitable for a dog. If a place is too small and too crowded, it's not worth putting him in a potentially bad situation. But if it's a place you love, you may be able to make special arrangements with management. Perhaps there's a place they can seat you that will be easier on your dog. Talk it over with the people in charge. If you are ever refused entry because of your dog, explain the Americans with Disabilities Act (ADA) and any local service dog laws. Try to educate rather than confront.

WORK

Taking your dog to work may be one of the main reasons you wanted a service dog. There may be many things that he can do for you to make your job easier—picking up whatever you drop, helping you up or helping you get around. But you need to make certain that it's a safe and healthy environment for him before you bring him there.

Spend a few days at your job looking at things from your dog's point of view. Is there a quiet, out-of-the-way place close to you where he can settle? Under the desk or in a corner is best. He will be resting most of the time and he needs to feel secure and comfortable. You might want to bring a rug or towel that becomes his bed for the day.

Do you have to leave your office frequently? If so, is it better for him to come with you or remain in your office? Is he safe staying there without you?

Is there a lot of traffic in and out of your office? Can you educate people not to feed him without your permission, not to tease or scare him, and not to play with him without your direction? Helen's dog became the "good luck charm" for students at the University of Arizona. They would come in before an exam and pet Nutmeg for luck. As long as they ask, everyone benefits.

Is there a place to take him out to relieve himself, and will you be able to find the time to do that every two or three hours? Don't count on someone else taking him out; it's your responsibility. It also gives you a break from work and a chance to be with your dog. That means rain or shine, so is there a protected place during inclement weather?

Is access to your workplace easy with a dog? Heavy doors and narrow spaces can be difficult. Do you have to walk a long way across a parking lot that might be very hot in the summer? If so, you might consider booties for your dog.

Think about your co-workers as well. If they are afraid of or allergic to dogs, work with them to come up with a solution. Try to work it out before your dog ever comes with you. Don't make it a confrontation. Remember that everyone has rights.

When you feel you have assessed the situation thoroughly and are comfortable that your dog will be fine at the office, bring him in on a weekend. Go through your routine and see how he fits in. Then bring him for half a day. Be alert to any stress he demonstrates, such as excessive panting or drooling or any other signs of extreme nervousness. Follow through on commands just as you would at home, making sure you show patience. Use praise and treats.

When you take your dog to work, it's important to find an out-of-the-way place for him to spend his time. You can either bring a bed for him to sleep on or make sure he's comfortable under your desk. Top—Bob Alan (osteoporosis, heart transplant) and Oinker (dalmatian/beagle/terrier mix) Bottom—Nutmeg (yellow lab)

Build up the time you have him at work—one day a week, then two or three days a week, then everyday. But there still may be times when it will be better not to bring him. If you're a tax accountant, April might be too stressful. If you work in a department store, "black Friday" or the day after Christmas might be a good day to leave him home. If you're a teacher, think about the first and/or last days of school. If your dog becomes frightened or overwhelmed, you may never be able to get him comfortable in that situation again.

SCHOOL

Taking your dog to school involves many of the same considerations as work. You should spend a few days going through your routine from his point of view. If you are a child taking a dog to elementary or middle school, have your parent or guardian accompany you the first few times you bring your dog. He should only stay through one or two classes to get used to the noise and confusion of so many kids.

Kellie, with juvenile rheumatoid arthritis, was in the fourth grade when she began taking her German shepherd, Atlee, to school. She and her mother arranged to do demonstrations for the teachers, staff, and student body before she began bringing Atlee regularly. Everyone learned how to behave responsibly around a service dog and how to help rather than hinder the process. The students also saw Kellie and her disability in a more positive light.

Change of class can be a difficult time. Students may be hurrying or running through crowded hallways. Make sure your dog is comfortable in crowds. Encourage him in a positive confident manner. Lunch is also difficult. Everyone must understand that this is a working dog and that he should not be fed, teased, or overstimulated. This is the kind of education you want to give in the demonstrations.

If you ride the school bus, try to arrange to practice getting on and off before the school year begins. Your school district will probably make arrangements. Talk to your regular bus driver so he or she can learn how to help. If you get on the bus via a lift, the driver may have to hold your dog while you get on or off.

If you are in college, look at the campus from your dog's point of view. One potential problem is that many college campuses have lots of dogs running loose. You must have confidence that your dog will not react aggressively toward other dogs. If a strange dog approaches you in an aggressive manner, your best bet is to release your dog if you're able. The two dogs will most likely sniff each other and not fight unless you interfere. If your dog is attached to your wheelchair you can try moving away from

Your dog must be very well behaved before you bring him to school with you. You will have to pay attention to your teacher so your dog must lie quietly beside you until you need him. Amy Heilig (cerebral palsy) and Krackers (golden retriever) with Hector Rodriguez (Amy's aide), Vivian Largent (teacher), classmates Becky Mills, Matthew Wallace, Brittney Rorex and Jennifer Goff

the other dog. If that doesn't work you should move into the other dog in a challenging manner, using your wheelchair as a weapon.

If you'll be on campus all day you must find the time and place to let your dog relieve himself. Most dogs that are fed on a schedule will have regular bowel movements. You can time this so your dog goes at home. If he does have a bowel movement on campus, you should pick it up if you are able. If you cannot, make sure he goes in an out-of-the-way place.

Taking him out to urinate several times a day is your responsibility. Don't ask someone else. Todd was busy at the library, so he had his girlfriend, Anna, take Manitou outside. When Anna, who is not disabled, tried to come back in the library, the security guard would not let her bring the dog in. This was certainly within his rights. A service dog only has rights when accompanying his disabled owner, so make sure you can find the time to take care of this responsibility yourself.

Practice taking your dog public places for short periods of time to get him used to crowds and new situations. Then take him to one class. You will have to pay some attention to him to make sure he stays down quietly despite the distractions. Don't take him on exam day. If it's a large class that bursts into laughter or applause, be ready to correct him if he jumps up at the disturbance. He'll get used to it, but don't expect perfection the first few times.

AIRPLANE

If you plan to fly with your dog it's a good idea to go to the airport once or twice to practice. There are many different sights, sounds and smells.

If you are normally ambulatory, but use an airport wheelchair when traveling, practice with your dog. Usually there are wheelchairs that you can borrow, so bring a friend who can push you through the airport.

You want to get your dog used to going through security, but you won't be able to proceed without special permission. See if you can contact the head of airport security and explain that you're training your dog. If that doesn't work, you can find metal detectors in most government buildings, and practice there. The security guard will usually need to run a hand detector over you and your dog. Introduce your dog to the guard in a friendly manner. Then give your dog commands he obeys readily to make him comfortable while the guard examines you both.

If you're able to, go to a gate where a plane has just arrived and ask if you might get on during the clean up. Sometimes the turn-around is too brief to allow this, but if there's time and you have permission from airport security, the gate personnel are happy to let you practice getting your dog on the plane. Talk to him as you go down the jetway and enter the plane. Practice getting him comfortable in the space around the seats. When you make your reservations, say that you're traveling with a service dog and ask for a bulkhead seat—there's more room for your dog. But just in case you're unable to get that row, practice entering another row. You should have trained your dog to back up because he will be more comfortable facing out and there's no room to turn around. (See chapter 8—Reverse.)

If you can't get to the gates, you can still practice in the baggage claim area. If it's crowded, stay around the perimeter while your dog gets used to the noise and confusion. Don't overwhelm him. If he seems stressed, move to a quieter area or leave.

When you actually travel, make your dog's well-being a primary concern. Feed him early or not at all that morning. Arrive at the airport early to make sure you get the seat you wanted. Allow him to have a little water, then take him outside just before boarding time to eliminate. If you have to change planes, try to arrange enough time to take him out again. Check with the airports you'll be arriving at to see if they have a dog-friendly area. Many airports do.

Flight attendants are generally helpful and considerate of your needs when traveling, but you must make sure that they and fellow passengers don't bother your dog or try to give him food. Mary was flying home from Hawaii and the woman in the next seat couldn't stop petting Sage, even at one point getting down on the floor with the poor dog. Mary finally asked her to stop so Sage could get some rest. Then, as they were getting off the plane in Los Angeles, Sage was lagging behind. When Mary turned to see why, she discovered that this same woman was walking down the jetway behind them holding onto Sage's tail.

You will probably have a fine time traveling with your dog as long as you prepare for the journey. It's not fair to just assume your dog will understand everything that's going on. He must have confidence in you and you must be considerate of him.

BARKING

The law allows anyone with a physical disability to keep a service dog in his or her house or apartment. Even if pets are not permitted, your dog has a legal right to stay with you. But just because the law gives you the right to have a dog, it doesn't give you the right to have a dog that is a nuisance.

Having a service dog and taking it places with you is, indeed, a right, but it carries with it a great responsibility. As we've said, you need to be responsive to and considerate of other people's feelings. You need to keep your dog under good control at all times. That even includes times when you're not with your dog.

Probably the complaint heard most often is from people who live near a barking dog. If your dog barks constantly and indiscriminately either when you're there or when you're gone, your neighbors are going to be annoyed. This holds true whether you're in a house or an apartment.

You've probably noticed by now that your dog has several barks. He barks differently for the garbage man, for a strange dog, for a person he knows and likes. He barks one way to play and another way to protect. Listen to your dog and you will hear many other tones as well. It helps if you recognize your dog's barks.

Some dogs bark indiscriminately all the time, but most bark at some stimulus. You owe it to your dog to check out what he's barking at. He's doing his job by alerting you to some situation he's aware of, but you then have the responsibility to demand that he be quiet.

But how do you get him quiet? If you yell, he's apt to think that the pack leader has joined in the barking. He won't hear your words. Your tone may tell him you're angry, but he will assume you're angry with the garbage man, too, so that just tells him that what he's doing meets with your approval. He barks, you bark. You've created a vicious cycle, and you must break the cycle to stop the barking.

You break the cycle by turning your dog's attention away from what he's doing. The easiest way is to make a different noise. When your dog looks to see what the sound meant, he will stop barking, even if it's just for a second. Then you must praise him "good quiet."

The noise you make must be loud enough and different enough to grab your dog's attention. One of the best sounds is from a "shake can." Take an empty soda pop can and fill the bottom with small stones. Tape the opening shut. When you shake this, it makes a noise that most dogs find unpleasant. It will penetrate through their barking, and they will look around to see where the noise came from.

Shake the can, drop it or roll it toward your dog. If the problem is outside-barking, hang the can outside with a string coming inside that you can pull when he barks.

Once you have your dog's attention and you have praised "good quiet," redirect his energy to a toy or a ball. If he returns to barking, repeat the noise correction and praise. Then try to get him interested in the toy or ball. This will take many corrections. For a dog that likes to bark (and many dogs are bred just for that) it will take time to recondition him.

When you can't be home you must find ways to keep him quiet. Many dogs become bored with long hours alone and they bark to relieve the monotony. Leave a radio or the TV on to keep him company. Give him one or two toys just as you're leaving. Say the same phrase every time you leave, such as "Be a good dog," "I'll be back soon," "Take care of the house." If you say the same thing each time, your dog will become used to your going away.

When you return, enter the house calmly and greet your dog quietly. Don't get excited or let him get excited. You want this to be a low-key experience.

If you have a problem, talk to your neighbors. One of them might be willing to visit with your dog while you're gone. Something to break up the boredom may be all that's needed.

CONCLUSION

It's becoming easier to have a service dog and take him to all kinds of public places with you. Public opinion continues to change as it becomes clearer how much assistance a service dog can provide for his disabled owner. This places a great responsibility on you. By taking this commitment seriously and keeping your standards high, you and your dog will be great ambassadors for service dog teams everywhere.

Chapter 5

PAWS
Teach your Dog to Put his Front Paws up on a Surface

Blake and his golden retriever, Savannah, frequent restaurants all over Tucson. When the meal is finished, Savannah's job is to take the check up to the cash register. She puts her paws on the counter and hands the bill to the cashier. This delights everyone. Unfortunately, at one of Blake's favorite restaurants, the bill is printed on flimsy paper so that by the time Savannah reaches the cashier it is a soggy mess that at least once jammed their cash machine. Rather than deprive her of a job she enjoys so much, the restaurant personnel all know to bring Blake two checks—one for Savannah to present to the cashier and one dry enough to go through the machine.

WHAT IS PAWS?

Paws is simply our word for a very useful exercise you can teach your dog. It means that your dog puts his front paws up on a surface so that you can reach him more easily. If you're in a wheelchair, you might want to teach him to put his front paws in your lap or on your footrests. If you use a scooter, you might want to teach him to put his front paws on the floor of the scooter. If you're ambulatory, you probably want him to put his front paws on a chair or table next to you. If your dog is small, you might want to teach him to put his paws very gently on you.

When your dog puts his front paws up on a surface near you or on your lap, he immediately becomes easier for you to reach. When he's retrieving objects for you, this may be the best way for you to take the object from him. If he's wearing a pack, this may be the only way for you to get things in and out. It's easier to put on his collar, halter, and leash this way, and it also makes petting, grooming, and giving affection much easier.

You can use any word you like. "Paws" and "lap" are the most common ones. Glenn tells his dog "biped." Lisa uses "pack." Be careful that the word you choose doesn't sound like another command or even have another meaning for your dog. For instance, if you use "up" for jumping up into the car, then don't use it here for putting front feet up.

There is one thing you need to be cautious of. If your dog demands a lot of attention from you, if he has a tendency to want to jump on you all the time, then do not teach him to "lap" directly on you. Teach him to put his front paws on a chair on your command only. Any time he tries to put his front paws on you, tell him "off" firmly. Putting his paws on you or furniture must always be at your direction. This is important for you to maintain leadership in your relationship.

TEACHING PAWS ON FURNITURE—
SANDRA AND CHANCE, HAROLD AND PRECIOUS

Sandra has arthritis and her husband, Harold, has arthritis and a heart condition. When Sandra lost her service dog, a bouvier named Hoss, they decided to rescue a bouvier puppy from Arkansas. They went to look at him and brought home not just him but also his brother. Harold's disability was getting worse and he realized that he could use the help of a service dog too. So they trained them together.

Bending over is difficult for both Sandra and Harold, so it was important to teach the dogs to put their front paws on a chair. Although bouviers are large dogs, it was still easier to have them up higher to put on the head halter and leash, to check their ears or teeth, and just to give them a hug.

Sandra was the more experienced trainer so she began first. With her dog, Chance, on leash, she approached a solid chair. Make sure the raised surface you use won't roll around or tip over. This will startle your dog and make him hesitant to try again. She held a treat against the back of the chair and patted it as she gave her command—both she and Harold use the word "rise." She coaxed and encouraged Chance with a happy voice, showing him the treat and then moving it to the back of the chair. The treat was just out of reach, so Chance put his front paws up to get closer and get the treat. As soon as his front feet were on the chair, Sandra praised with enthusiasm, "good rise," and gave him the treat. Sandra then pulled gently backwards on the leash and told Chance to get off. She uses "back" because that's the direction he has to move, although "off" is a good command here. Then she praised when his feet were back on the floor.

You can use any solid surface—chair, sofa, low table, fireplace ledge—any surface that's easy for you and comfortable for him. If you can't hold a treat, you can have a friend hold it over the chair. Either you or your friend can pat the surface to further encourage your dog. Make sure that the command and the praise come from you, and your friend should give you the treat to give to your dog.

If you have previously corrected your dog for getting on the furniture, be patient as you teach this exercise. He will probably be confused about what you're asking and will need lots of encouragement. You can still correct him if he gets on furniture without your permission. Teaching paws doesn't give him license to get up anytime he wants to.

Harold followed Sandra's lead and brought his dog, Precious, up to the chair. Precious was a little more hesitant and needed lots of coaxing. When he tentatively put one paw up, Harold praised enthusiastically and kept encouraging him. He tried to go around beside the chair to see if he could get to the treat that way. Harold just patiently brought him back to the front and continued to show the treat and move it back. Finally, Precious put both feet up, and Harold and Sandra both praised him and Harold gave him the treat.

Harold then told Precious "back" and pulled back on the leash so Precious got off the chair. Again, Harold praised, "good back." They then practiced two more times. Each time, Precious was a little quicker in his response. He was beginning to get the idea and he loved the attention and the treats.

After practicing for a week, Sandra and Harold then began to require their dogs to remain on the chair for longer periods. They petted them, adjusted

Having your dog put his paws up on a surface makes it easier for you to put on his collar and leash, get things out of his back pack, and check his ears. Sandra Schwartz (arthritis) and Chance (bouvier des Flanders), Harold Schwartz (arthritis) and Precious (bouvier des Flanders)

the halter, looked in their ears. They also practiced the command on different surfaces. Both Chance and Precious transferred easily to new places, and now will put their paws up whenever given the command. This is a very positive exercise. Sandra and Harold are generous with their praise, and there is still an occasional food reward to keep it interesting. It's a command they use a lot, and they want it to be a pleasure for their dogs as well as a help for themselves.

Always be aware of the surroundings when using this exercise. Make sure the floor isn't slippery and the surface for his front feet is solid. If your dog hesitates on this command, take him to the vet to be sure his hips are sound. Most dogs learn this command very quickly. Just remember that he should be doing it on your command, not whenever he chooses.

TEACHING PAWS ON WHEELCHAIR —ELAINE AND CHEEKO

Elaine has degenerative arthritis and uses an electric scooter to get around. She adopted Cheeko when he was a very small puppy, but he grew into a good sized lab mix. Starting from when he was small, she would have him ride on the scooter at her feet, so the scooter is something he's very comfortable with. If you bring an older dog into your home, you will have to get him accustomed to your wheelchair. Once he's comfortable around the chair, it's usually easy to teach this exercise.

Since Elaine is using a scooter, she needs Cheeko to come up onto the base at the side, not from the front. In a wheelchair, you might want your dog to put his paws on the footrests. Or you can teach him to put his paws right on your lap. In that case, he can approach it from either the front or the side.

Elaine held a piece of food in front of Cheeko and then moved it slowly across the scooter as she said "paws up." As Cheeko stretched after the treat, he put one paw on the base of the scooter and Elaine praised, "good paws up." She continued to hold the treat just out of reach until Cheeko had both paws on the scooter. She praised enthusiastically and gave him the treat. This took very little time to teach since Cheeko was used to riding on the scooter. If your dog is hesitant, just keep encouraging and showing him the treat.

Elaine decided she also wanted him sometimes to put his front paws on her lap to make it even easier to reach into his pack and adjust his harness and leash. She showed him a treat in her hand and raised it over her lap. With her other hand she patted her legs to encourage him to come up. As he reached for the treat, he put his paws on the scooter, but Elaine just kept coaxing him and patting her leg. He put one paw on her leg and she praised happily, so he put his other paw up. She said "good paws up" and gave him the treat.

Remember to give the command in a happy voice during this learning phase, but not so excitedly that he jumps up out of control. If you've been correcting your dog for jumping up on you, it will take longer to make him know that it's okay to come up gently on your command. You still need to correct him if he jumps on you without your permission.

If you can't hold the food, a friend can stand right behind you and hold the treat over your shoulder. Remember that you give the command, and praise your dog when he steps onto the scooter or into your lap. Keep encouraging him and enticing him with the food. As soon as he's in the position you want, give enthusiastic praise and have your friend give you the treat to give to your dog.

If you normally keep your treats in your lap, be aware that some dogs will use this as an opportunity to grab an extra piece of food. While teaching this command it might be wise to keep the treats out of his reach or have a friend hold them for you.

You can teach your dog to gently put his paws up on you, or on your scooter or wheelchair. Make sure it's on your command, not whenever he wants to jump up. Elaine Smith (degenerative arthritis) and Cheeko (lab mix)

Even little dogs can help a lot when they learn "paws." Helen Leavenworth (arthritis) and Frolic (pomeranian)

TEACHING PAWS ON YOU—HELEN AND FLUTTER

Helen has rheumatoid arthritis. She has always owned and shown little dogs, like pomeranians and papillons. Though Flutter is only an eight-pound papillon, Helen is teaching her to retrieve things she drops. Flutter is eager to please, and so as long as the object isn't too bulky or heavy, she's happy to bring it to Helen. The problem is that Flutter stands only ten inches off the ground, so Helen still has to bend way over to take the object from her dog. On some days this is very difficult, so Helen realized that teaching Flutter to put her paws on her legs would raise the object up.

Flutter, like most little dogs, likes to jump up on people. It's the only way they can get closer for attention. But this is not something you want from a service dog, even a small one. They could still hurt a child by jumping on them. Helen worked hard to teach Flutter the off command, so she would learn to keep all four feet on the ground. Then she began to teach her that it was all right to come up when a specific command was given.

Helen began working on this while sitting in a chair. All she had to do was pat her leg and say "paws" and Flutter was happy to put her front feet on Helen's leg. Helen gave her petting and praise, and sometimes a treat. Food wasn't really necessary because it was such a natural thing for Flutter to do. Any time that Flutter jumped on Helen without a command, Helen was consistent in telling her off. It's a fine line that the dog has to understand, but with patience and consistency, they can learn to distinguish.

Helen then worked while standing up. Again, you must be very consistent in always issuing the command before your dog jumps up on you. If he comes up on his own, say "off" firmly. If he doesn't get off immediately on your command, take a step into him as you repeat the command. Praise when all four feet are on the floor.

Every time she gave the command, Flutter was happy to put her front paws on Helen's knee. Helen then worked on making her remain quietly in that position for longer periods of time. Your dog shouldn't be jumping up and down against you; that's not the correct position. He should rest his paws gently against you and hold the position until you command him to get off. Praise and pet your dog. Hold a treat just above his nose while praising "good paws." Wait a few seconds before giving the treat. Continue to praise and wait a few more seconds; then command off.

Now, when Flutter brings anything to Helen, she obeys the paws command and gets the object closer to Helen's hand. With a small dog, you might also want to train him to hop up on the sofa next to you on command. That way when he is bringing you something, he can jump up and put it right in your lap.

PERFECTING PAWS

Practice this command two or three times a day under controlled circumstances. Make sure you are comfortable. Make sure the floor isn't slippery and that what you ask your dog to lap onto won't slip or roll away. Have food treats ready, but out of your dog's reach, and remember to praise with enthusiasm.

After several sessions where your dog quickly and correctly obeys both the lap and the off commands, try it without food. Give the command and pat the surface as usual. Praise as soon as he has his paws up. Pet him and adjust his collar or pack. Then command "off." He should obey readily. Praise again.

You probably won't have to practice this command because you will find that you use it regularly in your daily life. Each time he obeys, you must remember to praise him. Putting his paws up will become automatic, but he still needs to hear your approval. If you find he's anticipating and coming up on his own, be firm in your off command. Don't let him get away with this. He should only come up on your command.

Chapter 6

UNDER
Teach your Dog to Go Under a Table or Chair

Claire's large Irish setter, Tray, did very well going under tables and chairs, but when they attended the theater in New York there simply wasn't room for him. They were at the musical show "Cats" and a very polite manager informed them that the dog couldn't lie in the aisle, but she would be happy to place them in a box seat. As they gathered up their things to change seats, Claire overheard a woman behind them say, "Oh, a dog! I wonder how he's going to do with all these cats around."

WHAT IS THE UNDER EXERCISE?

The under exercise is teaching your dog to go under a table or chair. It's important that your dog be as inconspicuous as possible when you take him into public places. In restaurants he must get out of the way of waiters and waitresses. In movie theaters he must get out of the aisles. On airplanes he must occupy a very small space. If you teach him to obey the under command, he will readily move out of the way and learn to curl up in the space provided.

It's quite natural for dogs to go under things. They are "den" animals, meaning that their wild ancestors grew up and lived in dens. So as long as you approach this exercise in a positive manner and make him understand what you expect, your dog will find this perfectly normal, and it will make your excursions out with him much easier.

TEACHING UNDER—MORRIS AND SHANIA

Morris has severe back pain. After years of operating heavy machinery, he has three herniated discs, osteoporosis, osteoarthritis and a spinal column that is narrowing and compressing the spinal cord. It's nearly impossible for him to bend over, and he walks with the aid of a cane. Morris needed to teach his mixed breed dog, Shania, to go under a table without bending down to put her in place.

He began teaching the exercise using the dining room table, and his wife, Debbie, helped. She sat on the far side of the table as Morris and Shania approached. When they were at the edge of the table, Morris said "under" and Debbie called Shania. The table was tall enough that Shania could easily see Debbie and she went right to her. Morris praised "good under," then commanded her to lie down. She obeyed promptly because that was a command she knew well. Morris praised her, then he sat down at the table.

It's important to start at a table that your dog can get under easily. Ultimately you will teach him to go under low tables, even under chairs. But remember that you want to teach your dog what the word means in the most positive way.

Morris practiced several times, walking up to the table and always giving the under command as Shania was going under the table. Then he praised her for the under before he gave her the down command. After the first couple of times, Shania went under readily whether Debbie was coaxing her or not. They continued to practice at the dining room table for a week.

Morris next went to a low coffee table. Debbie sat on the opposite side with her hands underneath the table. Morris and Shania approached and Morris told her "under." Debbie called to her, clapping her hands to get

While teaching under it's helpful to have a friend on the other side of the table to coax your dog as you give the command. Morris' wife, Debbie, opens her hands in invitation. Morris Ardle (severe chronic back pain) and Shania (English pointer/lab mix)

Approach at an angle which forces your dog to go under the table; then turn out slightly. Give the command as he goes under and he will soon learn what the command means. Stewart Nordensson (cerebral palsy) and Laura (yellow lab)

Shania looking low. Shania had to get down and actually crawl, and both Morris and Debbie praised her enthusiastically. After several practice sessions, it was clear that Shania knew that the word "under" meant for her to go under whatever obstacle was there. They perfected the exercise by practicing at many different locations with many different tables. All work was done in a positive manner with as few distractions as possible.

TEACHING UNDER—JANE AND ZIO

Jane suffered a spinal cord injury from a fall when she was in college, and she uses a wheelchair. Like Morris, Jane chose her dining room table to teach this exercise. It's easy to approach and it's high enough that her labradoodle, Zio, would be able to go under it easily. She gave Zio a command to heel. As she approached the table at a 45-degree angle, Zio was between her wheelchair and the table. She moved in very close to the table so that he would automatically be forced under it. As they reached the table, Jane turned her chair just a little away from the table and continued moving forward about a foot. In this way, Zio was forced under the table as Jane gave the command "under." She stopped and praised "good under." He had no real idea what had happened, but after several times he began to associate the word with the concept of going under some obstacle.

If your dog hesitates or backs up as you approach the table, spend a little time getting him used to the table itself. Heel around it without going too close; walk up to it and stop a foot or so away and make him sit; heel toward it, then turn away. You should be talking to him in a high-pitched happy voice making this a joyous event. You can also get help from a friend who can sit on the opposite side holding a treat and coaxing your dog to come and get it. Remember, you should be the one to give the under command and the praise, but your friend can give the treat to your dog when he's under the table.

Zio didn't balk at going under the table. It was high enough that he could walk right under. But he did turn and move out before Jane could give him the down command. So the next time, she made sure that she had a short leash, and she gave the "down" command as soon as she praised "good under." Jane practiced several times coming up to the table and giving the command as Zio was guided under the table.

This method works very well in a wheelchair. You're using your chair to place your dog in the correct position. He goes under the table as a natural part of heeling. Be sure to give the under command as your dog is going under, so he learns to couple the word with the action.

When you move to a lower table, it might help if you are able to point under the table as you reach it. Your dog will probably have to get into a down position and then crawl under the table, so you will need to encourage him. It will help to have a friend with a food reward on the other side of the table. If you have practiced long enough at a high table so that your dog really knows what the word means, he should be able to make the transition to lower tables and chairs fairly easily.

USING UNDER

Once your dog has learned to go under any table any place, he will be an easy companion for you anywhere you go. Your dog will find the command comforting; he will feel at home in his den. If you go regularly to school or work, your dog will learn your routine and automatically go under your desk or table and fall asleep.

When you go to new places, you will have to assess the situation. At some restaurants the tables are too small for a dog to fit under. And keep in mind the size of your dog as well. Deb has a great Dane named Zapata that she takes wherever she goes. But it's not practical to think that a dog this big can ever fit comfortably under a table. Deb tries to find an out of the way table and then places Zapata as much out of traffic as possible. Use common sense and make the best of your circumstances. Usually, even if your dog can only fit partway under the table, he will be safer and more comfortable, and you can relax and enjoy your meal.

Chapter 7

SIDE AND FRONT
Teach your Dog to Move into Position Beside You or in Front of You

At the end of the recall exercise, the judge said, "Finish your dog." Lydia gave a crisp command, "Dinky, side!" Like she was on a spring, the little Aussie mix leapt straight up, turned in midair, and landed neatly and perfectly in a sit at Lydia's side. Smiling, the judge said, "Exercise finished."

Use the leash to guide your dog around into position as you teach the side command. Samir Madden (bilateral above elbow, bilateral below knee amputee) and Ashka (golden retriever)

Side and front are related commands. They both teach your dog to go to a specific position. Side will teach him to move immediately to your side and sit facing the same direction you're facing, ready to walk beside you or obey whatever command comes next. This is very useful whenever he's distracted and moves out in front of you. You don't want to trip over him when you start moving forward, and you don't want to have to adjust your position to his. He needs to learn to come immediately back beside you so that you can continue on safely.

Front will teach him to come and sit facing you. It's similar to side in that it's a position that you're teaching your dog. He already sits near you when he comes to you. Now you'll teach him that when he hears the word "front," there's a very specific place you want him to go to. This is helpful when he's retrieving objects, especially if it's difficult for you to grasp the object. It's also very helpful in teaching the "brace" command (chapter 12). When your dog learns to sit directly in front of you, you can use him to help you rise from a chair.

TEACHING SIDE

Ultimately when you give a side command, you'll expect your dog to move from wherever he is and come around beside you and sit. But he doesn't understand that yet. So you need to teach him what you want. In the teaching stages, you may have to move to get him moving.

As with all commands, the word you choose doesn't matter. Just pick one that doesn't sound like any other command and then stick with it. People commonly use "side," "around," "finish,"or "swing."

To begin, tell your dog to sit and praise for the sit. Tell him to stay and then pivot directly in front of him. If you're in a wheelchair, move away from your dog, turn, and then come back so that you are close facing him. If you heel with your dog on the left side, hold a treat in your left hand (if he heels on the right, substitute right side everywhere). Command "side" and then step or roll into your dog. He will be forced to get out of your way so he will be on his feet. Use the leash and the treat to guide him around to your left side. Praise "good side" as he's following the treat around. When he has turned so that he's facing the same direction you are, tell him to sit. Praise and give him the treat. Be sure to praise for the side as he's pivoting around.

If he doesn't turn, continue moving forward for a few steps so that he falls into heel position beside you. Praise "good side," then command sit. It's all right in the early teaching phase if you walk a few feet. Gradually you'll be able to use the treat and the leash to guide him around without you moving.

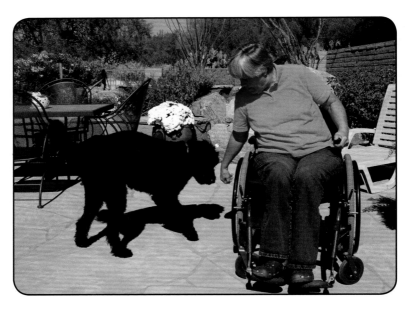

It's usually very easy to teach side using a treat to lure your dog into position. Jane Cords (spinal cord injury T-6) and Zio (labradoodle)

Use a food treat to bring your dog in close, then have him sit in front of you. Use a specific command, such as "front." John Cieslinski (multiple sclerosis) and Pepper (shepherd mix)

Practice two or three times in a row. Then work on other commands or play with your dog. Do the same thing in the next few practice sessions. Always give the command before you move into your dog. Remember you have told him to stay, so he needs to hear another command before he moves. Use the treat as a guide. Bring the hand with a treat around in a circle away from you and then back in beside you. If he follows the treat, he will pivot around and then be facing forward beside you. Praise as he's turning so he can associate the word with that action. Always tell him to sit if he doesn't automatically. That should always be part of the side command.

If you're unable to move your arms easily, then you'll have to use your body or your chair as the guide. Samir was born without lower arms, so he used his body and the leash to guide his golden retriever, Aska, around. He took a step forward as he gave the command which got her on her feet. Then he swung his upper body in a wide arc. The leash tugged her into the correct position. He then praised happily, "good side." Nancy used her wheelchair. She rolled very slowly into her labrador, Pupkin, as she commanded "side." She angled the chair so that when Pupkin moved out of the way, she would naturally move to the left side. Nancy praised "good side," then commanded "sit." Her husband, George, then gave her a treat to give to Pupkin.

After practicing for at least a week, see if your dog is getting the idea. Tell your dog to stay and pivot in front of him. Show him the treat. Command "side" and see if he gets up to move. If so, praise and encourage him to come around for the treat. If not, then move slightly into him to get him on his feet. And keep practicing.

Use other times to practice this. If your dog has wandered a few feet away, give your side command. He should respond by moving toward heel position. Use the leash and a treat to show him the correct spot and praise and encourage him. If you practice this consistently he will readily move to your side and sit facing the same direction you are. He will then be ready for whatever you tell him next.

TEACHING FRONT

Not everyone will want to teach their dog to sit in front of them, but there are many uses for this command. It can make it easier to put on a head halter. He's right there close so you can check his ears and teeth. And it may be the perfect position for you to teach him to brace to help you up.

Sit in a chair with your dog beside you. Hold a treat in front of his nose and move it around in front of you so he follows the treat. Say "front" as he gets in front of you. Praise when he's in position and give him the treat. Tell him to sit and praise for the sit. If he backs up and sits too far away, pull out another treat and entice him to come closer as you say "front," then "sit." Keep encouraging him until he sits in the position you want, which is very close to you, actually sitting between your legs. Praise "good front," and give him the treat. Practice two or three times. Be sure to use the command "front" so he knows this is a specific place.

Use treats every time for about a week so he comes to understand the place he needs to be for "front." Then taper off on the treats gradually. Continue to give praise and an occasional food reward to keep him interested. Always make sure you follow through on this command. If you tell him "front," then he must come and sit close, facing you.

PERFECTING SIDE AND FRONT

It's important to practice these commands regularly, even if you don't use them very often at first. They are good control commands, and they may come in handy later with other service exercises.

Practice side with distractions. Either set up the distraction or use those times when your dog is naturally distracted. Give the side command and follow through. You may have to move to get your dog's attention focused back on you. Be sure to praise as soon as he's in the correct position. If he won't look away from the distraction, use your verbal correction—"uh-uh-uh"—and walk away with him until you can get him to pay attention to you. This shows that you need to practice the exercise longer without distractions. You want to reach the point where you can say your command and he will immediately move to the position beside you without you having to move at all.

Once your dog is doing the front command well, you can practice it when you're sitting and watching TV. During a commercial, just call him to you and give the front command. He should readily come into position, even without food. If he isn't, then you need to practice longer, in a more formal way, until you're sure that he really understands what the command means. Remember, it's a position that you want him to assume whenever he hears the command. Don't let him get sloppy or you will have trouble later when you try to combine this with brace.

CHAPTER 8

REVERSE
Teach your Dog to Back Up

Claire finds it most comfortable to sit at a booth when she eats out. She quickly realized this was potentially a problem for her large Irish setter, Tray. He could go under the table but there was no room for him to turn around. Dogs like to see what's going on around them; they aren't comfortable with their backs to a room. Clearly, Tray was going to have to learn to back up under a table and then lie down, so they began working on the reverse exercise. A few days later, Claire's family took her out to dinner. She was excited to show them the new skill Tray had learned. They got to the booth and Claire commanded "back." Tray obediently took several step backwards under the table and everyone was impressed...until he ran his rear end into the center pole and with a surprised yelp that attracted everyone's attention leapt out from under the table. Claire was much more conscious of their surroundings from then on.

WHAT IS REVERSE?

This is one of the easier exercises to teach your dog, but it will take time to perfect. It can be very useful in many situations. It means that when you give your dog a command such as "back" or "reverse" he will actually walk backwards until you tell him to stop. This exercise is very convenient in restaurants where you want your dog to go under a booth table. Your dog will be more comfortable if he can face out, and some booths don't have enough space for him to turn around. If he can be taught to back into the space it will be easier for all of you. That's also true on an airplane and on school or city buses where the leg room is often restrictive. Backing your dog in will make the ride much easier.

Be aware that backing up is not natural for most dogs. They prefer to turn around and walk forward. They have to be very trusting of you as their pack leader if they are going to blindly walk backwards. This means you have to be aware of the obstacles they might run into. And you have to practice the exercise correctly. Make sure you're giving the command and praise while he's backing up. Don't allow him to turn around while you're giving the command or the praise.

TEACHING REVERSE

Whether you're ambulatory or in a wheelchair, teaching reverse is done the same way. The easiest way to teach it is to set up a barricade. You can use a wall and then set up some chairs parallel to the wall close together about three feet away from the wall. Or you can set up two rows of chairs about three feet apart. You can use two picnic benches set on their sides. You can use an existing barricade, like a coffee table and sofa. Just look around your house and decide what will work best.

John has multiple sclerosis. His shepherd mix, Pepper, is large, exuberant, friendly, and very eager to please. John knew he would need Pepper to back under tables to get out of the way. And he also planned to travel by plane with him. To be comfortable, he would need to learn to back into the row so he could face out during the flight.

John set up two rows of chairs in his living room. With Pepper on leash, he walked with him between the chairs until he came to the end. The chairs were spaced so that there was just room enough for them to walk between them. He commanded Pepper to sit, praised for the sit, then told him to wait while he pivoted in front of him. John was facing his dog, right in front of him.

John took a small step into him as he said, "Pepper, back." He naturally stood up and as John pressed forward, he took a tentative step backwards.

John praised excitedly, "good back," and took another step into him. Pepper tried to turn and move out of his way, but the chairs wouldn't let him, so he took another step backwards. Again, John praised happily. Then he turned around and walked forward with Pepper. They walked around the chairs, and then entered the narrow aisle again.

This time, John took a bigger step into him as he commanded "back," and he pressed him to move backwards. He used the chairs, his body, and the leash to prevent him from turning around. He took several steps in a row backwards. But as soon as he got to the end of the chairs, Pepper turned around. John realized he needed to stop before Pepper could turn around so he could praise for going backwards.

That's one of the most important things. You get overconfident because your dog is taking steps backwards. You think he understands the command. He doesn't. He's just getting out of your way in the only manner possible. You must practice faithfully many times before he will really know what the command means. Be sure you praise while he's backing up, not after he's stopped or turned around.

In a wheelchair, you can begin teaching it this same way. Turn in front of your dog at the head of the line of chairs and move your chair into him as you say his name and "back" or "reverse" or whatever command you want to use. He will certainly move out of the way of the wheelchair. Be careful not to come at him too hard and fast or he may panic and try to break through the chair barricade. You just want those chairs to act as a barrier, not a jail.

You may have to set the chairs a little farther apart to fit your dog and your wheelchair between them. This may allow your dog too much room to turn around when you move into him. If he can turn around, he will. Then he won't learn what you want. You can have a friend move the chairs closer together after you've moved through. Just leave enough space for your wheelchair as you go forward into your dog.

Nancy decided to teach her yellow lab, Pupkin, in a slightly different manner. Nancy has multiple sclerosis, and her husband, George, has always been a part of the training process. George set up the chairs far enough apart for Nancy in her wheelchair to move between them with Pupkin by her side. When they reached one end of the barricade, Nancy simply put her wheelchair in reverse and moved straight backwards. George placed himself in front of Pupkin so she had nowhere to turn around. As Nancy backed up slowly, Pupkin took steps backwards next to her. Nancy commanded, "Pupkin, reverse," as she started back. She praised for each step her dog took next to her, and George stayed right in front of the dog as they

When you use a barrier, such as chairs or a coffee table, your dog will back up easily and you can praise happily. Stop the exercise before he reaches the end of the barrier. John Cieslinski (multiple sclerosis) and Pepper (shepherd mix)

In a wheelchair, you can simply back straight up between the barriers. A friend can stand by to be sure your dog doesn't try to turn around. Nancy Mairs (multiple sclerosis) and Pupkin (yellow lab)

backed up. They only went a few feet, then Nancy stopped and moved forward to do it again.

After several practice sessions, George moved away to see whether Pupkin was learning the command. As Nancy backed up and said, "Pupkin, reverse," Pupkin took two steps backwards. Nancy praised "good reverse." But she continued to back up and Pupkin moved to turn around. Nancy gave a verbal correction—"uh-uh-uh," and she immediately stopped. She realized that she had asked too much for the first time without George as an added barrier.

George again took up position right in front of Pupkin and they successfully backed up several feet. After practicing this way for several more days, they tried it without George in front. Nancy went only a few steps backwards so she could praise Pupkin for obeying. Because Pupkin was really learning what the word meant, she began to progress rapidly.

PERFECTING REVERSE

After several weeks of practice, when your dog is moving easily backwards, remove one side of the obstacle. Give the command as you've been doing and take two or three steps (or roll a couple of feet) backwards. Your dog should readily step back, and you must praise happily when he does. If he immediately turns around, then he doesn't know the command yet and you need to practice more with the barricade in place.

Build up the distance you ask him to go backwards slowly. You can praise for each step and continue to give your reverse command. This isn't like saying "sit, sit, sit," to get your dog to sit. With sit, you wanted one action, so you gave one command. Reverse is a continuous action; every step backwards is "reverse," so you should issue the command more than once. And praise every few steps.

It will always be easier to get your dog to back up when it's in a confined space. Then it will make sense to him, and as long as you've taught him what the command means, he will be happy to comply. It's more difficult in a wide open space. Then it doesn't make sense to him not to turn around. But if you practice diligently, he can learn to move backwards for as long as you tell him to. Just remember to praise when he does.

Chapter 9

RETRIEVE
Teach your Dog to Take Objects and Give Them to You

Once a dog learns to retrieve, he generally loves it and tends to re-trieve everything in sight. Mike's shepherd mix, Ruby, brought him the newspaper, at first one torn page at a time, eventually in a more complete and readable form. Morris' mix, Shania, retrieved a pin cushion for Morris' wife, Debbie, and never got stuck. Christa's black lab, Sarabi, brought her the bedspread, in the living room. Lynn's golden retriever, Mr. Darcy, likes to retrieve toilet paper and proudly brought Lynn a new roll, in the middle of a party. Mary's golden retriever, Sedona, brought a desert tortoise into the house and kept nudging it through the living room while it hissed in protest. The prize might go to Pam's dog, Pluto, who arrived early one morning at her bedside with a full watering can, proudly holding it over Pam's head, dribbling water.

WHAT IS RETRIEVE?

Retrieve is the word that covers all actions relating to your dog picking things up for you. It includes picking up dropped objects, retrieving things at a distance, finding objects by name and carrying things both beside you and to another person. Retrieve is also the basis for many other service exercises, such as opening doors and helping you dress. It's probably the most difficult exercise to teach, but because of its many uses it's a most important one for your dog to learn well.

We offer three ways that people with disabilities have taught retrieve. Each method can take months to teach solidly. Even if your dog is a natural retriever, he needs to be taught the structure of the exercise so he does it readily and confidently on your command and not just when he chooses to. You may have to vary these methods or even devise your own. We simply offer ideas based on our experience.

This chapter covers the basic "take-hold-give" of the retrieve exercise. The next chapter teaches retrieving from a distance, retrieving by name, and carrying objects. Don't jump ahead. Your dog must know "take-hold-give" solidly before you move on. Otherwise both you and your dog will become frustrated. Remember that slow is fast.

You must be very careful not to become angry and scream at your dog if he picks up something and runs with it. If you yell at him for picking things up it will be more difficult when you begin teaching the retrieval. If he does pick up something he shouldn't, call him to you, entice him with food or a toy, and calmly take the object. If possible, praise him for picking it up and bringing it to you. If he doesn't bring it and you have to go and get it from him, do it calmly. You don't want retrieval to ever have negative connotations.

Before you begin, you need to have a picture in your head of exactly what you are going to do each step of the way. It will be helpful if you read this entire chapter first and keep it handy while you practice. Remember that you are teaching in small increments. Don't push ahead too fast or you will sacrifice precision. This is the basis for so much of your future training that you need to teach it solidly. So read the chapter, think it all through and then progress slowly and surely, and you will be rewarded with a dog who works for you readily, happily, and with confidence.

TAKE-HOLD-GIVE—MARY AND SAGE

Mary prefers to teach this exercise by "successive approximation." She rewards her dog with praise and treats for each small step forward. She knows exactly what she expects her dog to do and she pays very close attention so that she can praise the second she gets the correct response. Timing of the praise is very important in this method. He must hear immediate praise in order to know what you want. Remember how you praised him the second he assumed the sit or down position so he could learn what the word meant? It's even more important here because the exercise is taught in sections, and your dog must understand each section in order to progress.

Mary spends time getting prepared to practice this exercise each time. She sits in a chair and puts several treats on a table within reach. She puts her dog on leash and wraps the leash around her leg so her hands are free, but her dog can't wander off. She gets her specific take-it object in her lap.

You may want to try different objects for take-it until you find one that your dog prefers. Then stick with that one item. Make it something easy for you to hold, perhaps a wooden dowel, a piece of plastic PVC pipe, or a rawhide bone. Mary likes to use the cardboard roll from inside paper towels or toilet paper. It's readily available and easily replaceable, plus it helps your dog learn to have a soft mouth and not chew on the item. The object you choose then becomes a training tool and he isn't to have it unless you are working with him on the retrieval exercise. Always put the take-it object away between practice sessions.

During training sessions, if the object falls you must be able to pick it up again. Keep a long-handled reacher nearby or make a small hole near one end of the object, place a loop of string through it, and put the string around your arm.

Although Sage was a golden retriever, retrieving was not natural for her. She didn't play ball or other retrieval games and she resisted take-it. Mary used a paper-towel roll. Her idea for the first step was simply to have Sage look at the object when given the take command. She held the roll right in front of Sage and said "take it." Watching carefully, Mary praised "good take it" when Sage looked at it. Then she gave her a treat. She did this three times in a row praising Sage just for looking at the roll.

The next day Mary wanted Sage to actually touch the roll with her mouth or nose. She waved the roll in front of her while saying "take it" in a happy voice. She then held it right in front of Sage's nose and held a treat on the opposite side. As Sage moved toward the treat her nose touched the roll and Mary praised enthusiastically and gave her the treat. She did the same thing twice more, then put the object away. Two more times that day they practiced the same routine.

The next day, Mary held the object in front of Sage's nose without a treat behind it. She gave her take command in a happy voice. Sage was required to touch the object before receiving praise and a treat. It was no longer sufficient to just look at the object. Sage responded by putting her nose

Spend time getting prepared to practice take-hold-and-give. Treats should be within reach and your dog should be on leash and close to you. Praise for each small step as you teach this exercise. Mary George (rheumatoid arthritis) and Sedona (golden retriever)

on the roll. Perhaps she was looking for the treat, but whatever the reason she gave the response Mary was asking for. So Mary gave immediate and excited praise along with a treat. Remember that your timing here is very important. You need to be quick with your verbal praise, even if it takes you a few seconds to get the treat to your dog.

If your dog doesn't touch the object on his own, try waving it around in front of him. Then bring it right up to his mouth. You might have to do this several times before he touches it on his own. Practice only three times in a row two or three times a day.

Mary stayed at this step for several days. Each time Mary held the object and said "take it," Sage was expected to touch the roll. When she did, she received praise and a treat. The next step is for the dog to open its mouth for the object. Mary worked on this by teasing Sage. She brought the roll right up to Sage's mouth, then pulled it away in a playful fashion all the while saying "take" in a happy voice. Now it was no longer enough for Sage to touch the object; she would have to take it in her mouth.

This may take longer to achieve. If you keep it light and happy most dogs will automatically open their mouths as the object comes close. Keep trying these positive, play techniques. It's much better for your dog to figure out what you want and then be rewarded for that process than to be forced into an action.

With the happy teasing, Sage responded by opening her mouth as the roll came toward it. Mary gave very enthusiastic praise—"good take." Sage immediately spit the object back out and Mary quickly said "good give." Mary did not let go of the roll so she was ready to repeat the sequence in the same playful manner. Sage again opened her mouth and Mary praised and gave her a food treat. Then she put the object away and they practiced other things.

This begins the long process of perfecting the take-hold-and-give. Once your dog is opening his mouth, it's still a long way to a solid retrieve. You must teach him to willingly receive the object every time. He must then learn to hold onto that object as long as necessary. He must give the object to you on your command.

Mary practiced daily at this stage for several weeks. Sage began to anticipate the object coming toward her and she opened her mouth to receive it. Mary held onto the roll and praised for the take. If Sage held it in her mouth even for a second, Mary praised, "good hold." If Sage seemed inclined to chew the roll Mary said, "uh-uh-uh" and pulled the object out saying "good give."

Then Mary held the roll about six inches from Sage's face and gave her the take command. Because they had worked long enough Sage reached out for the roll and took it. Mary's praise was especially exuberant and she gave a jackpot of treats. This showed that Sage was really learning the command; she understood that "take" meant to put the object in her mouth and she was willing to reach for it.

If your dog doesn't reach at this point, you must continue working at putting the object into his mouth. You might try another method, such as more play (see next section).

Mary was encouraged by Sage's response to reach out and take the object. Now she wanted to teach her to hold it in her mouth. When Sage took the roll, Mary rubbed under her chin and said "good hold." After a second or two she said, "give" and took the object. She praised verbally but withheld the food reward. Sage was used to getting a food treat immediately, which made her anxious to spit out the object to get the treat. Now Mary wanted her to learn that she would get food eventually, but first she had to hold onto the object until Mary told her to give. Gentle rubbing under the chin encourages your dog to keep his mouth closed and to lift his head, which will make it easier for you to take the item from him.

Mary practiced two more holds that session. Then she gave Sage a food treat and put everything away. They had two more sessions that day. Each time Mary required Sage to hold on a few seconds longer, continuously rubbing under her chin to encourage her. If Sage spit out the object before Mary said "give," Mary would correct with a gentle "uh-uh-uh." She then picked up the roll and repeated the take command. Sage wanted to please and was beginning to understand what produced a positive response and what produced a negative response. She began holding on long and longer and receiving Mary's enthusiastic praise.

At the same time, Mary began making Sage reach farther and farther for the object. She held it to the left; the next time she held it to the right; then she would lower it a little toward the floor. If Sage hesitated, Mary went back a step until she got a positive response. She then worked at that level several times before holding the object away again.

Ultimately you're going to want your dog to pick things up from the ground. Build up in stages by holding the object a few inches below his mouth, then a few inches lower. Put the object at the edge of your couch and tell him to take it. Keep your hand on one end at first. Then try it without holding the object at all. All of this may take weeks to achieve. Don't rush. Take the time to teach each step thoroughly.

One way to gradually lower the object to the floor is to place the object on a stack of books just a little lower than your dog. Do several take-its at that height over a period of a few days. Then remove one book and practice at that level several times. As you remove each book, the object moves closer and closer to the floor and your dog will naturally be able to make the adjustment.

By the time Mary actually dropped an object on the floor, Sage had learned the command so completely that she immediately picked it up and brought it to Mary's hand. Mary praised quietly and reminded her to hold it. When Mary could grasp it, she said "give" and praised with great enthusiasm. Don't say "give" too soon or your dog will drop the item on the floor. Make sure you're in position to take the object from him to make this a successful exercise.

Practice each step thoroughly before you move on, and be prepared to back up a step or two if your dog seems confused. If you build up slowly and teach this exercise positively, your dog will come to enjoy retrieving everything you drop.

RETRIEVE IN PLAY—CHRIS AND KOA

Some dogs are very resistant to learning a formal take-it, but that doesn't mean they can't learn to retrieve. If you have reached the point where you want to pry open his jaws or wring his neck, take a totally different approach and work through play.

Chris is quadriplegic with limited arm strength and movement. His young Australian shepherd, Koa, was not making progress using traditional methods, so Chris decided to try using his dog's natural enjoyment of play retrieval games. If your dog isn't retrieving a ball or a toy, spend some time encouraging him to enjoy these games. Stop all formal retrieval training and concentrate only on play. Toss a ball and chase it yourself to encourage him to go after it. Throw soft toys and Frisbees and nylabones until you find something that excites him. Once you find the object that he will chase, it becomes a training tool. Keep it out of sight except when you bring it out for play. If he absolutely refuses to retrieve in play, see the next section of this chapter.

The first thing Chris had to do to play retrieval games was to teach Koa to place the ball on Chris' lap. Koa would drop the ball on the floor in his excitement to have it thrown again, but Chris can't reach the floor. He needed Koa to place anything he retrieved on his lap.

When Koa dropped the ball on the floor, Chris had a friend give the ball back to Koa—not throw it, just put it in his mouth—while Chris patted his lap and said "bring it here." If Koa dropped the ball again, the friend gave it back to him. He was not getting the reward he wanted, so eventually he put the ball on Chris' lap. Immediately, he received very enthusiastic praise, and Chris threw the ball, which was the ultimate reward. With a dog who loves to play ball, it only takes a few times before he understands that the only way to continue the game is to place the ball on your lap.

When Chris tossed the ball, he encouraged Koa as he ran out to get it. Chris used a series of words in conjunction with the play, all said in an excited happy voice. Koa was not expected to pay attention to the words while playing, but he would gradually come to associate them with the formal commands later.

As soon as Koa started after the ball, Chris called "find it!" The moment Koa put his mouth on the ball, Chris said "take it." As Koa began returning with the ball, Chris said "hold," as he encouraged Koa to come to him. It wasn't a formal recall, just part of the game. When Koa reached him, Chris praised with great enthusiasm, patting his lap and saying "bring it here." As Koa released the ball, Chris said "give."

Chris repeated this exact sequence each time he tossed the ball. This takes practice. It can be difficult getting it all straight with exact timing. Expect to get flustered and a bit frustrated at first, but don't give up. Concentrate

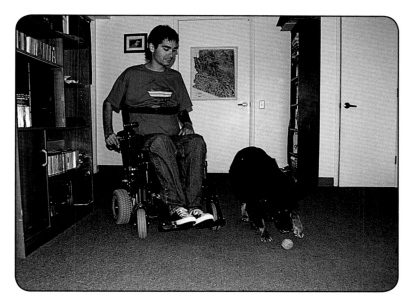

Use the words for "take-it" in a happy, excited voice when teaching retrieve through play. Your dog won't even know he's learning but he is. Chris Wenner (spinal cord injury C 5-6) and Koa (Australian shepherd)

on using the same words while having fun. It will all come together.

All this time Koa was hearing the words take, hold, and give as part of a play routine he thoroughly enjoyed. He had no idea he was learning a command, but he was. Be sure that you don't issue the words in a command tone of voice in case your dog refuses to pick up the item.

After several weeks of this play, Chris tied a cloth around the ball and threw that. Koa ran out to get it and brought it right back. Chris praised him enthusiastically and threw it several times. They practiced with this object for a few days. Then Chris took just the cloth and threw it while using the same encouraging play voice he'd been using all along. Koa went after it and brought it right back. If your dog simply sniffs at the object, encourage him using a happy voice. If he refuses to pick it up, go back to the cloth wrapped around the ball for a while and then try again.

Chris then began dropping the cloth rather than throwing it, but still using the same happy play voice to encourage Koa. Koa didn't realize it, but he was learning to retrieve. He picked up the cloth and gave it to Chris because it was fun. Chris dropped the cloth in different places, sometimes throwing it, sometimes just dropping it. Each time he was enthusiastic and happy, and Koa became adept at picking it up. Just dropping an object is not as exciting to your dog as when you throw it, so you have to make up for that with the enthusiasm and joy in your voice and your body language. Let your dog know that this is really fun! If you believe it, he'll believe it too.

Over the next few weeks, Chris began dropping other objects and using the same happy tone to keep Koa interested in retrieving them. Each time Chris would praise with delight and often give a food reward. He began to put more command and less play in his voice, but he still kept it upbeat and happy for both of them. In very short order Koa was willingly retrieving everything.

The problem that Chris discovered with this method was that he didn't have a solid hold. When you make it a game your dog will tend to toss you the object quickly in his excitement to have you throw it again. The easiest way to get a hold command is to make it part of something else.

When your dog goes out and gets an object and brings it to you, he is, in fact, holding the object. You need to encourage that by putting a word to it. As he comes back to you, tell him "good hold" in a happy voice. When he gets to you, tell him "hold," and don't take the object right away. If he drops it, use a verbal correction—"uh-uh-uh"—and command him to take it again. It takes a little work but he will learn what brings praise and what doesn't.

You can also combine hold with carry. When your dog has the object, give him a heel command and start walking. If he drops the item, have him take it again and start off again. Praise if he only takes a step or two beside you holding the object. If you have help from a friend, you can teach your dog to carry to another person (See next chapter). He is learning the hold every moment that he keeps the object in his mouth while concentrating on something else.

RETRIEVE FROM FLOOR—STEWART AND MARIA

If you have difficulty holding onto items, you may want to try Stewart's method. Stewart was born with cerebral palsy and trained dogs since he was a child. He used many different methods over the years. He had to work out this method with his young standard poodle, Maria, because she was very resistant to learning take-it, and Stewart could not throw things in play as Chris did. This method is a long process that requires great patience.

He first worked through in his mind what he would need to do and then got everything ready. He used a friend as a training tool and told her exactly what he wanted her to do. He also explained to her what he was going to have Maria do. He put the collar and leash on Maria and got treats and his retrieve item ready to go.

He chose to use a small towel as his take-it object. He pushed the towel off his lap and said, "take." This wasn't a command; it was just a word that he wanted Maria to associate with the towel falling off his lap. The second she looked at the towel he gave her enthusiastic praise and a small treat. His friend Zenona put the treat on his lap and he gave Maria permission to eat it. Stewart gave all the commands and the praise. Zenona then picked up the towel and put it back on his lap.

They did this three times, then put the towel and treats away. In a few hours he set everything up again exactly the same way. He did this for several weeks. Every time he pushed the towel off his lap Maria would look at it and get praise and a treat. If she didn't look at it, she didn't receive any reward. Zenona simply picked up the towel and they tried again.

After several weeks he didn't give her a treat when she looked at the towel. He kept encouraging her to "take" in a happy voice. She looked at the towel and looked at Stewart for her reward. When it didn't happen, she put her nose on the towel. Stewart gave her lots of praise and many treats— a jackpot.

Stewart knew that her touching the towel might have been just a coincidence, but he was now going to insist that she touch the towel before she was rewarded. He did it immediately again, hoping that she would associate the jackpot of treats with this new requirement. She put her nose on the towel as soon as he dropped it, and he again praised her enthusiastically and gave several treats. After the third try, he put everything away. He practiced at this level two or three times a day for several days.

Stewart then dropped the towel and withheld food and praise even though she touched the towel. When she didn't get a response, she picked up the towel. Stewart gave lots of praise and a handful of treats—again, a jackpot for a big step forward. She was making progress in learning the command. This didn't mean she now picked up the towel every time. If she ignored Stewart's command, he would tap the towel with his foot while encouraging "take it." If she continued to ignore it, Stewart's friend picked up the towel and they tried again a few minutes later.

As Maria became more consistent in picking up the object, Stewart felt that she knew what the word meant, so he began saying it in a more commanding way. He still kept his voice happy and encouraging, but it took on a more serious tone.

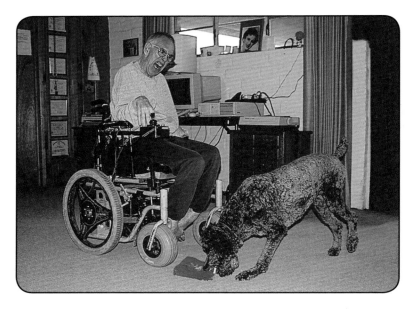

Simply dropping an item will take much longer to teach, but as long as you use lots of praise and food rewards your dog will learn to retrieve anything you drop. Stewart Nordensson (cerebral palsy) and Maria (standard poodle)

The next step was for Maria to learn to put the towel where he could reach it. Because Stewart had muscle spasms, he couldn't always quickly grasp an object and he needed his dog to place the item on his lap. He again withheld treats and kept encouraging her to pick up the towel and place it on his lap. Somewhat in frustration she plopped it into his lap and he was lavish with praise and treats. After a few weeks of practice Maria was regularly placing the towel in Stewart's lap, and he began giving treats at random rather than every time.

It may take several practice sessions, possibly even months of work, to get your dog to place the item where you want it. You must have patience and keep working in a positive manner. If you're using a food treat that he really wants, he will eventually figure out what gets him the reward. Keep praising and encouraging your dog for each small step forward. Remember that slow is fast.

Next, Stewart had Zenona take the towel and place it about four feet away. Maria had to learn to go and get the object and bring it back. She understood the command well enough that she didn't hesitate to go for the towel. Although she dropped it on the way back, she picked it right back up again and gave it to Stewart. Zenona moved the towel farther away, eventually putting it in another room for Maria to find.

Stewart also began working with different items. He put a handle on the telephone to make it easier for her to pick up. He put a piece of cardboard on his ring of keys because Maria, like many dogs, did not like to pick up metal. She learned to get these objects and bring them to Stewart. He knew he had a great helper the first time he dropped his towel by accident when he and Maria were alone. He commanded take and she picked it up immediately and gave it to him.

PERFECTING TAKE-IT

You will have to practice retrieve for several months, even when your dog is picking things up readily. You want to use many different objects and practice in different places in addition to your house. Begin in each new location as if it's a brand new exercise. He needs to learn to retrieve things quickly and directly, even with distractions. Build up slowly to give you both confidence.

Then you can move on to other service exercises that require a solid take-it. Practice each exercise thoroughly and you will soon have a dog who is helping you in many important ways.

Chapter 10

RETRIEVING AND CARRYING
Teach your Dog to Retrieve Objects from a Distance,
Find Objects by Name, and Carry Objects

In addition to teaching Manny to pull him in his wheelchair, Todd also taught her to retrieve his wheelchair by pulling a strap on the frame of the chair. She loved to pull him along when he was in the chair; she was less thrilled to pull the empty chair to him. One evening as they were moving along through a parking lot toward Todd's truck, the wheelchair hit a bump and Todd fell out. The chair rolled away about twenty-five feet. Todd was unhurt but he was alone and his chair was out of reach. He told Manny to get the chair. She pulled it toward him, but she'd never been asked to pull it that far. It didn't roll straight and would twist to the side. In frustration she came back to Todd repeatedly. He praised her and again told her to get the chair. She gamely went back and was able each time to bring it a little closer. After nearly half an hour, Manny triumphantly pulled the wheelchair within reach of Todd. He gave her a big hug and she seemed to smile with pride, and relief.

RETRIEVE FROM A DISTANCE

Retrieving means that your dog will pick up objects either beside you or at a distance. If you taught him take-it using the play method, he already goes out to get things when you throw them. He will also learn to go and get things that you point to or items that roll under a table or chair. Certain things he will learn to retrieve by name. He can also learn to carry things beside you and to another person. Continue practicing your take-it by dropping the item farther and farther away from your dog and encouraging him to go and get it.

When he is reliably retrieving objects that you toss, the next step is to put him on a stay, go about six feet away, and drop the object. Go back to him, praise for the stay, release him and say, "take it." Point toward the object and move toward it if your dog doesn't go right out to get it. Encourage him to take it and bring it back to you. He needs to hold onto the object until you can take it from him. If he drops it, tell him to pick it up again and concentrate on teaching him hold. Practice this retrieving from a distance until you have a solid response each time. You will probably want to combine it with naming certain items as taught in the next section.

RETRIEVING OBJECTS BY NAME

This can be a very helpful exercise and it's simple to teach once your dog is retrieving things on your command. There are many different applications; you just have to decide which items your dog must learn by name.

When your dog is reliably retrieving items from the floor, take a specific item—the phone, your keys, the remote control, your shoes, your cane, whatever you would like him to bring to you—and begin to work exclusively with that item for a while. Give it a name as you drop it. Don't just say "take it;" say, "take keys." Say that every single time, and praise with "good keys." Practice for a week or two. Then place the keys along with two other items on the floor. Command, "take keys." If he goes right to the keys, then you know he knows its name. If he hesitates, encourage him, using the word "keys." If he picks up the wrong item, just say "uh-uh-uh" quietly and try again. Then go back to working with just the keys for another week. Be sure you use the name each and every time and praise with enthusiasm.

You can do this with every item you want him to bring to you. Work with each object separately until he really knows its name. Move the object to different places. Begin within sight of the object and gradually move farther away. In time, with patient training, he can bring you your shoes in the morning, your slippers in the evening, the remote control and the telephone whenever you need them.

Once your dog learns what the word "phone" means, he can find it wherever you might leave it and bring it to you when you need it. Zio (labradoodle)

TELEPHONE—MARY AND SAGE

Things have changed quite a bit since Teamwork II first came out. Cordless phones were the rage then; today nearly everyone has a cell phone, and they keep it clipped to them or carry it in their pocket. So it may not be as necessary for your dog to retrieve the phone as it once was. But it's still a useful exercise in case you need your phone and it's not within reach.

Mary used to miss a lot of phone calls. She's had rheumatoid arthritis since she was two years old. It affects nearly all of her joints and she uses a lift chair to help her up. Because it took so long for her to get to the phone, people would hang up, so she decided to teach her golden retriever, Sage, to get the phone on command. Mary put a handle on her cordless phone to make it easier for Sage to grab it. Your cell phone is smaller and easier for your dog to hold, but be aware that it may slip out of his mouth. You might want to train using an old cell phone so your good phone doesn't get damaged. And if you keep the phone in some kind of a case, it will be easier for your dog to grip it.

Mary didn't want Sage to respond to the phone ringing; she wanted her to get the phone on Mary's command only. This was for two reasons: if Mary wasn't home, she didn't want Sage getting the phone when it rang, and if Mary fell and needed the phone quickly, she didn't want to wait for it to ring before Sage would bring it.

After Sage was picking up everything Mary told her to, Mary began working exclusively with an old telephone. Mary pointed to the phone and said, "take phone." She named the object every single time and praised with "good phone." Remember that you can use any word to name any object as long as you're consistent in using the same word for the same object every time. Blake claims that when he first told his golden retriever, Savannah, to get the phone, she got her bone instead. So he chose a totally different command. Blake says, "Ring! Ring!" and Savannah goes and finds his cordless phone.

After working for a week with the old phone, Mary changed to her real phone. She was sure that Sage would now bring it without dropping it. After getting Sage used to picking up the real phone from the floor, she placed it on its cradle, and moved about six feet away. She pointed toward it and said "take phone." Sage hesitated so Mary moved toward the phone repeating the command. Sage then went directly to it. You must be sure the phone is accessible to your dog when it's in its cradle. Sage was easily able to grasp the handle and bring the phone to Mary. Mary praised enthusiastically and gave her a jackpot of treats.

If you leave your phone in different places, you must train your dog to find it and then bring it to you. Practice by putting the phone on differ-

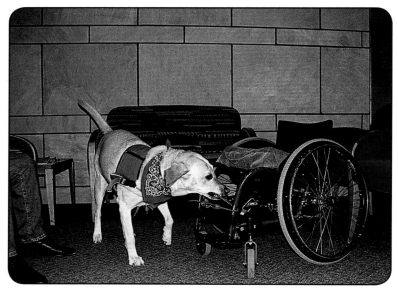

A wheelchair is heavy and awkward for your dog to retrieve but with patient practice he can learn to grab a strap or cord on the front and pull it to you. Nutmeg (yellow lab)

Even little dogs will happily bring you your shoes or anything else you teach them to retrieve by name. Patch (jack russell puddin)

ent surfaces around the house. Start close to the phone so you can point to it and walk toward it if your dog hesitates. As he gets the idea of what you want, move out of sight of the phone and command "take phone" in a happy excited voice. Keep encouraging him to search for it. Praise with enthusiasm and lots of treats if he finds it and brings it to you. If he doesn't, then keep practicing within sight until he really knows what you want.

WHEELCHAIR—HELEN AND NUTMEG

Teaching your dog to pull something like a laundry basket or your manual wheelchair by holding a strap in his mouth involves several skills—take and hold, reverse, and pull. For your wheelchair, put a small strap somewhere in the front so the chair will roll forward.

Helen injured her spinal cord in a bicycle accident when she was 14 years old. Her wheelchair is lightweight and apt to roll away. She wanted her yellow lab, Nutmeg, to learn to retrieve it for her, so she wrapped a bungee cord around the front of the chair.

She told Nutmeg to take the strap and she played with it to entice her dog. Helen made sure the chair didn't roll at this time. She wanted Nutmeg to get used to putting the cord in her mouth. When Nutmeg grabbed the strap, Helen praised her and told her to hold it. As Nutmeg became proficient at grabbing the strap, Helen began using the command, "take the chair" and encouraging her to grab the cord.

Once, as Nutmeg tried to bring the cord to Helen's hand, the wheelchair moved forward. Nutmeg was startled and immediately dropped the strap. Helen told her to take it again, and praised and encouraged her. As the chair rolled a few inches, Helen praised. Then Helen took the strap, praised enthusiastically and gave Nutmeg a jackpot of treats. They practiced with the chair moving a few inches for several days. Nutmeg got used to the movement of the chair as she retrieved the strap. But she never liked it. Be patient with your dog as he works this exercise.

Next Helen pushed the chair about a foot away. This was simply a matter of Nutmeg holding onto the cord and pulling it toward Helen. When the chair was moved about six feet away, Nutmeg had to use the learned skill of backing up while still holding onto the strap. If she turned sideways, so did the wheelchair. So Helen gave the command "take the chair," and as soon as Nutmeg had the cord, Helen told her "back." (See chapter 8—Reverse). She took several steps backwards, pulling on the strap and the chair followed. Don't be surprised if your dog drops the strap to obey the reverse command. He'll have to be taught that he must do both things at once.

Helen and Nutmeg had to practice for several weeks before this process became smooth. A wheelchair is heavy and awkward and difficult to pull straight. You will have to figure out what works best for your dog to grab. It will take innovation and teamwork to make this exercise successful for you.

CONCLUSION

You can use this procedure with any item you want your dog to retrieve for you regularly, and he can learn the names of several different objects as long as you use the names consistently. Mike wanted his white shepherd mix, Ruby, to bring his shoes. She enjoyed it so much that she would try to take them off his feet so she could retrieve them. Carlos taught his rottweiler, Josh, to find and bring his cane from wherever Carlos left it. Nancy's little Jack Russell terrier, Patch, races into the bedroom to retrieve Nancy's shoes. Sometimes he brings them one at a time and sometimes both together.

You must practice faithfully to teach your dog to identify and find specific items. All of your practice should be positive. If he brings the wrong item, don't scold. Just repeat the name of the object and encourage him to find it. If he consistently brings the wrong item, then he hasn't learned the name and you must go back to square one and build up slowly and solidly. It's important to do it correctly. As always, remember that slow is fast. Teaching him to bring you something like the phone is more than just convenient; it may save your life.

CARRYING OBJECTS

As you work with your dog on retrieval he is naturally learning to carry an object, but you will now need to teach him to carry on your command and under specific circumstances. If you drop a piece of mail as you come back from the mailbox, you may want your dog not just to pick it up, but carry it to the house for you as well. If you drop a sock with your arms full of laundry it will be easier for you if he picks it up and brings it to the washing machine. The ultimate joy for Mary was when Sage carried a basket of flowers down the aisle on Mary and Kevin's wedding day.

Once your dog has a solid take-it, you can begin working on carry. Use an object that he takes readily. Give your take command and praise as soon as your dog has the item in his mouth. Then give your heel command and start forward. He may drop the object as he moves with you. Stop, have him take the object again, and repeat the heel command. You may have to do this several times. If your dog takes even one step with the item in his mouth, praise him and keep going. After a few feet, stop and have him give you the object. Praise and give him a food reward.

Once your dog understands what's expected, he will usually carry any item for you for as long as you need. Remember that dogs need to pant in order to stay cool, so don't ask him to carry things for long periods, especially when it's hot. Don't ask him to carry heavy or awkward objects for any distance. Some objects may get caught in the wheels of your wheelchair and you may have to teach him to heel a wider distance from the chair when carrying such items.

CARRY PERSON TO PERSON—KELLIE AND ATLEE

If you live with someone else—spouse, parent, child, roommate—you may want to teach your dog to carry objects to and from that person. Kellie has juvenile rheumatoid arthritis. When she was younger and living at home, it was difficult for her to go from the family room to the kitchen because of several steps. That meant that her mom was always bringing her sodas and snacks. When Kellie began training her German shepherd, Atlee, one of the skills the family wanted Atlee to learn was to carry things from person to person.

After Atlee was consistently retrieving objects on command, Kellie began working on having her carry those items while walking beside her. Then Kellie and her mother, Patti, stood a few feet apart. Kellie gave an object to Atlee and said "take it to Mom." At the same time, Patti called to Atlee. The first time, Atlee dropped the item and went to Patti. Patti ignored her and Kellie corrected with a verbal "uh-uh-uh." She told Atlee to pick up the item, which she did; then Kellie repeated "take it to Mom." Again Patti called and this time Atlee went to her carrying the object. Both Kellie and Patti praised Atlee, and Kellie gave her a treat.

They practiced this for a week, standing only a few feet apart until Atlee was doing it correctly each time. Over the next several weeks, she learned to take from either person and carry the item to the other. Kellie and her mom moved farther and farther apart until they were on opposite sides of the room. Atlee thought this was a fun game.

Next, Patti stood just outside the room out of sight while Kellie gave Atlee the item and said, "take it to Mom." Patti called and Atlee came right to her and gave her the object. Patti then gave it back to Atlee and said, "Take it to Kellie." Each time she delivered the object she received lavish praise. They practiced this over the next few weeks, moving to different parts of the house. Atlee showed that she had learned the total concept by going immediately to the other person without being called.

The next thing to solve was how Atlee would carry an open can of soda

To teach your dog to carry something from one person to another both people must be enthusiastic. Begin close together and gradually move farther and farther apart. Kellie Christenson (juvenile rheumatoid arthritis) and Atlee (German shepherd)

to Kellie. They found a narrow basket that just held the can without letting it tip over. Kellie taught Atlee to hold and carry the empty basket without mouthing it. Then she put an empty can in the basket and had Atlee carry that several times. Next they used a half-full can of soda and finally a full can which was considerably heavier. Atlee learned to carry the basket without spilling the soda, and it became the most used item in the household. Whenever Kellie wanted a soda, she gave Atlee the basket and sent her to Patti. Patti opened the soda, put it in the basket, and sent Atlee back to Kellie. It saved wear and tear on everyone, and Atlee loved being part of it.

CONCLUSION

Teaching your dog to carry from person to person can be a big help in your daily routine and will be fun for him. You can also teach him to carry objects to another place. Nancy often drops laundry items on the way to or from the washer. Her terrier, Patch, has learned to follow behind her and pick up anything that drops. He carries these items either to the laundry room for Nancy to put in the machine, or into the bedroom where she folds the clean laundry. He even jumps up on the bed with the item and proudly gives it to her for folding.

You can teach your dog to take an item and drop it in another place—such as dirty clothes on the floor into a hamper. Simply tell him to take the item and carry it beside you. Walk to the hamper and tell him to drop it. Use a word, such as "laundry" or "hamper" in conjunction with the commands he already knows so he will learn this is a specific repetitive action. You can do the same with trash that you have him put in a wastebasket and his toys that he puts away in a box. Remember to praise and reward him with a food treat. When you make it fun for your dog he is happy to help in many ways.

Your dog can help in so many ways, especially on laundry day. Patch picks up any clothes his owner drops. Pepper loves to take the clothes out of the dryer and hand them to his owner.
Left—Nancy Martindale (spinal stenosis/lupus) and Patch (jack russell puddin)
Right—John Cieslinski (multiple sclerosis) and Pepper (shepherd mix)

Chapter 11

FIND A PERSON
Teach your Dog to Find a Person if You Need Help

Pam has spinal muscular atrophy, and she was teaching her dog Pluto to find her husband, Brian, for those times when she might need help. Pluto was enjoying the training—she loved to go bark at Brian and have him respond and follow her back to Pam. One day Pam was lying in bed and began to vomit. In serious danger of choking, she wasn't even able to whisper to Pluto. Without a command, Pluto went right to where Brian was working in the garage. But this wasn't a training session. Brian might have simply said hello to the dog and gone on with his work. Fortunately, he sensed something in her behavior and went to find Pam. He was able to help her sit up to prevent choking. Brian and Pam were very grateful that they had been practicing this exercise, and they were astonished at Pluto's instinctive response.

Remember how Lassie would go for help whenever Timmy got in trouble—which was just about every week? Well, you can teach your dog to do the same for you, and just like Lassie it could save your life. It's easy to teach even if he doesn't know any other service exercises, so you can begin right away. It's also fun to teach, kind of a game for everyone involved.

You will have to decide whom you want your dog to learn to find—your husband, wife, parent, child, or roommate. If you live in an apartment complex you might work with a neighbor who is willing to come when needed. How you teach this will depend on the location of the person that your dog will be finding. If that person is within your house, your dog will learn to go to that person and make contact. If the person lives in a guesthouse or another apartment, your dog will have to find a way to alert that person. The person who is helping you must be an enthusiastic and willing partner.

As with all the exercises in this book, we offer some ways people have taught their dogs. These are just ideas to help you. You may need to figure out your own method depending on your circumstances.

GETTING HELP—NANCY, GEORGE AND PUPKIN

Nancy has multiple sclerosis. She's a noted author and a very active person, but sometimes she needs help from her husband, George. Her voice is soft, so she can't count on George hearing her if she is calling in an emergency. They wanted to train their yellow lab, Pupkin, to find George whenever commanded to do so.

George took a treat and walked a few feet from Nancy and Pupkin. Nancy said in a very excited voice, "Pupkin, find George!" As soon as she gave the command, George called to Pupkin showing the food. Pupkin ran to George. He got very excited and said, "Pupkin, where's Nancy?" Then he ran over to Nancy with Pupkin. He gave the treat to Nancy and she gave it to the dog. Both George and Nancy praised Pupkin.

They repeated the sequence twice more. Everyone was laughing and happy and Pupkin thought it was great fun. She, of course, had no idea what she was doing right, but she knew something positive was happening.

The important things to remember are to give a "find" command to your dog. The person being found should call your dog in the early stages, so he knows he's supposed to go to him/her. Then the person should consistently say some phrase to your dog in an excited voice. Then he/she should come immediately to you. Your dog will come along because he will see that there's a treat. Both people should praise the dog and you give him the treat. How your dog alerts will depend on you and your dog—you can have him bark or make physical contact, something that gets attention. John and

Most dogs love the "find" exercise. It brings all their people together. Remember both of you should praise your dog. Nancy Mairs (multiple sclerosis) and Pupkin (yellow lab)

Norma needed their rottweiler mix, Magic, to go find either one of them on command. They both have back problems and either might fall and need help from the other. He was happy to go find either one, but he didn't bark naturally, and since he regularly came to both of them for affection and attention, they couldn't tell if he was coming because the other person had sent him or if it was just a time to be petted and loved. So John and Norma both carried a bandana with them at all times. If John fell and needed Norma's help, he would tie the bandana on Magic's collar and send him to Norma. She would see the bandana and know this was serious. Magic would then lead her to John.

Nancy and George chose to use a target touch with this command so George could differentiate the times when Pupkin was just coming to say hello and the times when Nancy needed him. George put his hand in front of Pupkin's nose. When she touched it out of curiosity, he said, "good find," and gave her a treat. They practiced faithfully for several weeks. Nancy would say, "find George," and both would praise when Pupkin touched his hand.

Nancy and George practiced "find" twice a day for several days. George moved farther away each time. After four days, he went into another room so that Pupkin had to actually find him. He called her as soon as he heard Nancy give the find command, and she came right to him. He praised with great enthusiasm and they both went back to Nancy. After several successful attempts, Nancy gave the find command but George stayed silent. Pupkin came to the place they'd been practicing. As always, George asked, "Where's Nancy?" and they went back to Nancy together. The next time they practiced it, George went to a different place. Pupkin actually had to look for him. When she found him, he got very excited and let her know she had done a great job.

Some dogs will realize that they can get a treat just by bringing you both together. It's always best to respond in case it really is an emergency. But if you find your dog alerting all the time without a command, don't reward those times. He only gets praise and treats when he's been given the find command.

Nancy and George also had a small problem with their older dog, Bentley, who had been taught to find George. Initially Bentley would lead Pupkin in the search for George, so they put him in another room for a few practices. Pupkin then got the upper hand/paw. Now she races ahead of Bentley to be the first to find George. They found that the competition actually enhanced the process, but in the early teaching stages, you may need to remove one dog to allow the other to learn.

Practice this command often. Have the person move from room to room, hide in closets and behind drapes, and even go outside. In the early stages the person should call your dog to encourage him to find him/her. Soon your dog should be searching for him/her without any extra help. Have fun with this command, but realize how important it might be. Even when he thoroughly understands the command, continue to practice occasionally just to keep him sharp.

GETTING HELP—STEWART AND COQI

Stewart hired someone to live in the guesthouse on his property to help in the evenings and weekends. His dogs could go out through a doggie door at will, so it was easy for them to learn to go to this person if Stewart needed help. But if the person was inside the guesthouse with the door shut, how would he know that the dog was trying to reach him? This will also apply if your dog must alert a neighbor.

Stewart worked out two different methods for his dogs—barking and ringing a bell. If your dog is not a natural barker, bell ringing is much easier to teach.

Coqi was a Belgian tervuren and definitely a natural barker, so Stewart just used her natural tendencies to teach her to bark on command. Whenever she barked, he said, "Speak, good speak." In time he could say the word first and she would respond by barking. Stewart and Jim, the resident of the guesthouse, talked about exactly what they were going to do. Because timing is important, make sure that both you and the person to be found understand what you plan to do, what you expect of your dog, and how each of you needs to respond.

Stewart had Jim hold several treats. He then gave Coqi a compound command: "Speak; find Jim." As soon as she barked Jim put a treat on Stewart's lap. Stewart gave enthusiastic praise and let her have the treat. They practiced this routine three times a day for a week.

Then they all went to the guesthouse. Stewart and Coqi set up outside with Jim just inside the open door. Stewart gave the compound command. When Coqi barked, Jim came out rapidly and put a treat on Stewart's lap. Stewart gave praise and let her have the treat. They practiced this three times a day for another week. Coqi quickly understood what was expected and she was already barking before the first session was over on the first day. Because Stewart wanted to really instill it in her in case he had an emergency, he took time practicing before moving on to the next step.

At the beginning of the third week Stewart sat about five feet away from the door of the guesthouse and said, "Find Jim." Coqi immediately made a dash for the door and began to bark like crazy until Jim came out and put a treat on Stewart's lap. If your dog doesn't automatically start for the door, you can move toward it as you repeat the command excitedly. He should respond at this point or you need to go back one step and continue practicing right at the door.

Stewart kept moving farther away from Jim's door, practicing each stage for several days, until he got to his backdoor. Every time he moved back a few feet he would give the command and Coqi would race over and bark. If at any point your dog seems confused and doesn't respond promptly, go to the door with him to make sure you get a correct response. Check to see if there is some major distraction. Work close to the door several times before you move away again.

The next stage was for Stewart to stay in his house and command Coqi, "find Jim." The very first time he gave the command Coqi went flying out the pet door, went over to Jim's backdoor and jumped up and down while barking until Jim came out. She continued barking as Jim came into Stewart's house and put a treat on his lap. Stewart gave enthusiastic praise and let her have the treat.

Stewart practiced sending Coqi for help from every room in his house at all times of the day. He began giving treats at random. Then he had Jim come in and speak to Stewart for a few seconds before he praised her. If there ever were a real emergency no one would be able to pay attention to her. Stewart wanted her to get used to waiting.

Stewart and Jim practiced this regularly. It was fun for Coqi; she liked both of them, and because she was a herding breed it was natural for her to want them together. Jim learned to recognize when Coqi was just out in the backyard barking and when she was barking at his door. He always remained alert and responded every time.

GETTING HELP—STEWART AND MARIA

Stewart's next dog was a standard poodle named Maria. She didn't bark very often so Stewart needed to find an alternate method to alert Bob, who was then living in the guesthouse. He found a heavy metal hanging bell and placed it just outside the door of the guesthouse within Maria's reach. The bell needs to be heavy so that it doesn't ring with the slightest breeze but not so heavy that your dog can't make it ring.

To teach Maria to touch the bell Stewart handed Bob several food treats. Stewart said, "Maria, find Bob." Bob held one treat behind the bell. When Maria tried to reach around to get the treat, her nose hit the bell. It rang and Stewart gave enthusiastic praise. Bob then put the treat on Stewart's lap for

Maria to have. The ringing of the bell is actually reinforcement for your dog to know he's done it right. In this early stage, you must praise for the slightest contact with the bell, even if it doesn't ring, so be very alert.

Stewart and Bob practiced three times in a row two or three times every day. By the end of the week Maria was beginning to work out what got her the treat. Bob stopped holding the treat near the bell. Stewart kept encouraging her, "find Bob." She looked at Bob and the treat and then touched the bell. Stewart gave very wild praise and they gave her several food treats—a jackpot for figuring out what was expected. If your dog doesn't get it yet, then move the treat near the bell until he touches it and keep practicing at this level.

They continued to practice several times a day until Maria was consistently ringing the bell on command. Then Bob went inside his house and shut the door. Stewart and Maria came out near the house and Stewart said, "find Bob." This was the first time Bob hadn't been present and Maria was a little confused. But because they had practiced long enough she touched the bell. Bob immediately opened his door and spoke to Maria: "Does Stewart want me?" He then took a treat over and put it on Stewart's lap while Stewart praised Maria.

Beginning to teach "ring the bell." Stewart praises enthusiastically as soon as Maria touches the bell.

For the next step Bob was inside his house and Stewart and Maria were about five feet from the door. They continued practicing while moving farther away each time. Maria responded correctly, going over and ringing the bell. Bob always came out quickly as soon as the bell was rung.

Then Stewart and Maria sat just inside Stewart's house with the backdoor open. Stewart gave the command to find Bob. At first Maria just looked at Stewart, so he started outside as he repeated the command. This time she went right to the bell. Again, Bob came right out and spoke to her as they went over to Stewart. This is an important part of the training. The person being alerted needs to speak to your dog in a happy enthusiastic way and needs to come to you with your dog. You then praise and give a treat.

The next stage was for Bob not to respond instantly as Maria rang the bell. If Maria came back toward Stewart without Bob, Stewart would repeat the command. She learned to keep ringing the bell until Bob came out. Then she received her praise and reward from Stewart.

After several successful repetitions at this stage, the next step is for you and your dog to be inside your house, and the person being alerted inside his or her house. Tell your dog to find the person. By now he should respond quickly and correctly, going right to the bell. If not, you need to go back several steps and keep practicing until you get a prompt response.

You may find that your dog goes out and rings the bell without a command, just hoping to get a treat. The person being alerted needs to respond and come to you, but if you hadn't commanded your dog, then he should receive no praise or food. Just ignore him and go on about your business.

Remember that you won't know when you'll need this command, but when you do you will really need it. Make sure your dog thoroughly understands and performs it without hesitation. Continue to practice regularly so that if it's ever needed your dog will be ready to help.

Chapter 12

BRACE
Teach your Dog to Support You to Help You up

Blake wanted his golden retriever, Savannah, to learn to come to him automatically to help him up whenever he fell. He practiced noisy falls on his wood floor using the crutches' clattering as a signal. As he fell he would call Savannah and praise when she got to him. She was so strongly bonded that it took little time to teach this. In fact she became so responsive to his being on the floor that it made it very difficult for Blake to read his Sunday paper. He prefers to stretch out on the floor with the paper, but every time he got down Savannah came running over to help him up. Wanting to reinforce her training, he would use her to help him up, thank her, and then get back down on the floor. She, of course, came right back to help. He finally realized he had to teach her another command. He used "I'm all right," meaning that it was okay for him to be on the floor. She would then let him read his newspaper in peace.

WHAT IS BRACE?

When we use the term "brace" in connection with service dog exercises we are referring to the dictionary definition: "to support or hold steady." This means that you will teach your dog to assume and hold a position solidly, so you can lean on him in such a way that it will help you. You might be able to use your dog to help you get out of a chair, get up from the floor, transfer from bed to chair, or support you up stairs or curbs.

This may be a very helpful exercise for you. It's amazing how just a little steadying can make all the difference. If you are at all unsteady on your feet, your dog can provide support just by you putting your hand on him. It's a simple act that might keep you from serious injury.

CAN EVERY DOG HELP?

The answer is an obvious no. If you would like to lean on your dog to help you get off the floor, how much help can a miniature poodle be? If your dog is old or frail, you cannot put weight on him. If you are very heavy, no dog will be strong enough to truly support you, although he could help steady you if that's all you need.

So the size and condition of the dog is critical to the success of this exercise. Even if you only want your dog to provide you with a little balance, your dog must be tall enough to be helpful. If you plan to put any weight on him, he must be big enough, strong enough and healthy enough that you won't hurt him.

When you lean on your dog, you put great stress on the point where you're leaning. Once you teach your dog to stand solidly while you lean on him, he will maintain the position even if it hurts him. His dedication to you and your needs will frequently outweigh his own discomfort, so you have to be continuously aware of his condition and be responsible for him. We recommend that you consult with your vet before you begin this exercise. Tell him/her specifically what you want to do and check to see if your dog will be able to do it.

It's very important that you do this exercise correctly right from the start. You must never lean on your dog's back or head. You must use his shoulders. That's the strongest area of a dog's musculature. You can use his head or back lightly to provide stability, but never put weight on either area.

It's also important that your dog stand solidly with legs about shoulder width. If his legs are too close together or he is in an awkward stance, he won't be able to support your weight.

Teach your dog to brace solidly and he will be able to help you up when you fall. Top—Blake Gigli (spinal cord injury T 12) and Savannah (golden retriever) Bottom—Diane Manchester (multiple sclerosis) and Mojo (labradoodle)

TEACHING BRACE

There are many different ways that you can use this exercise. You must think about your individual circumstances and decide the best way for your dog to help you. We will recount here several ways that people have taught their dogs to brace; you can use these ideas to work out the best way for you.

What you are trying to teach your dog is that when you say a word, such as "brace" or "help me," he will respond by stiffening his body to prepare for your weight. If you were to lean on your dog right now, without any command or any training, he would either lie down or run away. He needs to be taught what you mean by the command, and he must get his muscles conditioned to support your weight.

When you practice, be sure to work on a surface where your dog's feet won't slide. It's hard for him to help you if he can't keep himself up. Let your dog find the position most comfortable for him. If he shifts position when you first put pressure on him, give him the opportunity to get comfortable before you increase the pressure.

BRACE FROM THE FLOOR—BLAKE AND SAVANNAH

Blake is a paraplegic from a plane accident and gets around mostly on crutches. He sometimes falls and getting up is hard for him. He decided to teach his golden retriever, Savannah, to provide support. He began by having her stand in front of him while he sat in a chair. He put his hand lightly on her shoulders, slightly off center, saying, "brace." He pressed lightly downward and inward, at first with just enough pressure for her to be aware of his touch. He praised and removed his hand. Then he gave his release word.

Savannah had no idea what was happening, but she naturally began stiffening as the pressure increased. Blake never put so much pressure on Savannah that she would be tempted to move away. He didn't need to. All he was going to ask of her was that she stand solidly while he used her for balance as he got up. He praised her as he felt her muscles stiffen and gave her an occasional treat. Gradually he increased the pressure.

Blake wanted Savannah to stand next to him when he fell. This was the best position for his circumstances. You may want your dog in the sit position. If so, simply command "sit" with your dog in front of you, and place your hand on his shoulders. Say, "brace," and push down slightly. Increase the pressure gradually, so your dog gets used to it. You want to feel his muscles stiffen up. That's when you praise, "good brace." Then remove your hand as you release your dog.

Your dog will learn to stiffen up when he hears the brace command. Then you can lean on him enough to help you get up out of a chair. Helen Mendelsohn (back and cranial nerve damage) and Hope (German shepherd)

Blake taught Savannah to come to him automatically whenever he fell and stand close by in front of him. He put his hand on the far side of her shoulder and commanded "brace." Before putting any weight on her, he checked the position of her legs to make sure they were far enough apart to support him. He pushed off from the floor and used Savannah for balance.

It didn't take Blake very long to teach Savannah to help him up because it was something he needed regularly. It's an easy exercise for most dogs. You just have to be patient and take the time needed to teach your dog to stand or sit solidly when you lean on him. Remember not to put too much weight on him; just use him for temporary support. Be sure to place your weight over his shoulders.

BRACE FROM A CHAIR—HELEN AND HOPE

You might want your dog to help you get out of a chair, simply leaning solidly on his shoulders and pushing yourself upright, using him like the arm of a chair. Put the minimum amount of weight on your dog to allow you to get up; don't lean heavily on him. Be sure your hand is on his shoulder, not his back or head.

Helen, who has back problems, frequently needs help from her German shepherd, Hope, to get out of a chair. If the chair is low or has no arms Helen sometimes finds it difficult to stand. She taught Hope to turn sideways to her and sit. She used food to show her the position, and then she praised when Hope was there. Each time, she made sure that Hope was sitting comfortably so that she wouldn't move once the brace command was given. You can also teach this by having your dog stand in front of you as Blake did. With either position, be sure your dog is solid and not slipping on the floor.

Helen then gave a brace command and placed her hand directly on Hope's shoulder. She put light pressure and praised when she sat solidly in front of her. She practiced several times a day, slowly increasing the amount of pressure as Hope got used to sitting rigid.

The first time she practiced actually standing up she made sure she was in a chair that was easy to get out of. She also asked her Dad to stand by in case Hope moved suddenly and knocked Helen off balance. She got Hope in the proper position in front of her and gave the brace command as usual. Then she pushed herself up using the chair as well as Hope's shoulders. Hope started to move out of the way, but Helen gave a gentle "uh-uh-uh," and repeated the brace command. Because they had practiced so much, Hope remained solid while Helen stood up. Helen then praised and released her.

Make sure your dog remains in position until you are fully upright. If he moves away too soon you might lose your balance. So if he starts to move, repeat the brace command firmly. Praise as you put pressure on and rise slowly. There will be many times when you need this help so make sure your dog thoroughly understands the command.

KELLIE AND ATLEE

There may be several reasons why leaning on your dog won't be useful to you. Mary and Kellie both have rheumatoid arthritis. There's no way they could put weight on one arm to push off, so they found a way to use both arms.

Kellie was a small ten-year-old working with a German shepherd named Atlee. Mary was helping her train her dog, but it was the student who taught the teacher, as Kellie devised this method for both of them to use.

Kellie sat in a chair and commanded Atlee to sit directly in front of her, facing her. (See chapter 7). She used food to show Atlee where to sit. It was important that she sit quite close, actually between Kellie's legs. Kellie praised for the sit. Then she gave the command "brace" and reached both hands around Atlee's neck. The first time, she simply touched the back of Atlee's head praising "good brace." Then she released her.

Kellie had to practice both the front and the brace. She praised each time Atlee sat correctly and also praised as she put her arms around her neck. Kellie began to pull slightly toward her as she commanded "brace." Atlee tried to put her head down, but Kellie brought her muzzle up, repeated "brace," and put her arms around her neck. On the third try, Atlee kept her head still. Kellie praised quietly—"good brace"—as she put gentle pressure low on the back of Atlee's neck.

Gradually Kellie increased the pressure. Kellie was very light, but she still made sure that she put her hands low on Atlee's neck almost down to her shoulders. It's important not to put too much stress on your dog's head or neck.

Kellie practiced for a week and began to feel Atlee stiffen her neck muscles as she gently pulled. Be sure you softly praise your dog for this response. You want to teach him that the correct response to all that pressure is to remain solid. Continue to practice until he is responding to the brace command itself.

Next, Kellie actually used Atlee to help her up. She gave the brace command and pulled. She used her legs to help her push off, putting a minimum of pressure on Atlee. She praised her for staying solid. When she was standing, she released Atlee and told her to sit beside her. Your dog will have to get out of

It's important to place your hands toward your dog's shoulders. Then he will brace while you pull yourself up. Mary George (rheumatoid arthritis) and Sedona (golden retriever)

your way as you're getting up, but you don't want him to move too soon. So continue to occasionally practice just the pulling on your dog without actually getting up. Praise when he stays solidly in position. Then release him with an appropriate command.

STAIRS, CURBS AND RAMPS

If you are unsteady when you try to go up or down stairs, your dog might provide just the support you need. The most important part of this exercise is that your dog must have a very controlled "heel." (See the chapter "Controlled Walk" in Teamwork.) Practice on level surfaces to teach him to walk quietly beside you at your pace. Don't attempt to use him to steady you until he's very steady himself.

You might find a harness is helpful in this exercise if your dog is tall enough that you can grab the harness easily. If not, you may find that just putting your hand very lightly on his shoulders will steady you as you go up or down a surface. It's very important to remember not to put any pressure at all on your dog's head. You can very easily do serious injury to his neck.

If you use a harness, you may just want to hold onto it and steady yourself as you walk beside your dog up the ramp. Or you may want to teach him to actually pull you up. (See chapter 14, specifically "Pulling out of a Chair.")

To go up or down stairs with your dog, you will probably need him to go up one step and then stop while you use him as support. Use the harness or lean gently on his shoulders. Practice on one or two steps, like back steps at your house, to teach your dog to wait for you. The first time you try it on a longer staircase, make sure it's a quiet place without too much traffic, and bring a friend along.

For a curb, you may use your dog for balance as you do on stairs. Kellie found that she could use Atlee just as she did to get out of a chair. She had Atlee go up on the curb and sit facing Kellie. Then she wrapped her arms around her neck and pulled herself up the curb. This worked because Kellie was small and Atlee was quite large.

Going down off the curb, you will probably find that just leaning gently against your dog, and/or gripping the harness, will provide enough stability for you to make it safely. Remember to give your dog the brace command. This will remind him to provide solid support.

BALANCE WHILE WALKING—BOB AND CALYPSO

Bob has Parkinson's disease and epilepsy. Sometimes he has trouble walking. He will often freeze up or lose his balance and stumble. He used to fall all the time, and he still falls occasionally. When he does, his Belgian sheepdog, Calypso, is right there to help him up. But even more important, Calypso can prevent Bob from falling.

Calypso wears a leather harness that includes a stiff, strong handle. Since Calypso is a large dog, the handle is at a perfect height for Bob to grab it whenever he feels himself tilting or losing his balance. He will command Calypso to brace, but even if he's unable to get the command out, Calypso has learned that when he feels the pressure on the handle, he just stops and stands solidly. It may take time for Bob to regain his equilibrium. During this time, he will be pulling upward on the handle to keep himself from falling over. No matter how long it takes or what awkward angle Bob pulls at him, Calypso will remain stiff and solid. This has saved Bob from falling more times that he can count.

You may not need quite this much steadying when you walk. It may be that just a hand placed on your dog's shoulders will provide enough support to keep you walking straight. Your dog must be tall enough, and he must have a solid controlled walk beside you. As you're walking, place a hand

You may find a harness with a handle is useful when you walk. Your dog will learn to recognize when you need his support. Be careful not to lean too heavily on him. Bob Ruskin (Parkinson's disease, epilepsy) and Calypso (Belgian sheepdog)

Never lean too heavily on your dog when you transfer.
Skip Heyne (multiple sclerosis) and Brandy (golden retriever mix)

on his shoulder with a command such as "steady" or "balance" or "brace." At first put almost no pressure; then build up slowly. You will feel your dog stiffen against the pressure, and he will soon come to realize that you are putting your hand on him for a specific purpose. It may be just the support you need.

SITTING UP IN YOUR CHAIR—TODD AND MANNY

Perhaps your disability makes it difficult or impossible to straighten up by yourself if you lean over too far. This was a problem for Todd, who injured his spinal cord in a fall. Because of the weakness in his back, he needed a way for his lab mix, Manitou, to help him get back upright.

It's simply a variation of brace. Todd taught Manny to come to a certain place directly in front of him. You might prefer your dog on one side if one of your arms is stronger. Based on your circumstances you must decide the best place for your dog to learn to brace. (See chapter 7—Side and Front.)

Todd taught brace as in all the examples by gradually increasing pressure on her shoulders. He didn't need to put much pressure on Manny; it was simply a matter of having her serve as a solid surface so he could push off to sit upright. The most important part was just teaching her to stand rigidly in a specific place. Very soon Todd could feel Manny stiffen up when he said "brace" and placed his hand on her shoulders. Just that little bit of help made an enormous difference in his life. He no longer worried about bending over and being unable to get back up.

Stewart needed even less help. Just a finger pressed on the neck of his yellow lab, Laura, or in her collar, was enough to help him sit straighter in his chair. He taught her to sit beside him. On his brace command, she stiffened her body to receive the pressure. It's hardly noticeable, but it made a big difference for Stewart.

TRANSFER FROM CHAIR TO BED—JIM AND CODY

You may need help transferring from your wheelchair to a bed, another chair, the car or the toilet, and your dog may be able to help you. Remember that you can't put all your weight on your dog, but you might be able to use him to provide just enough support to effect the transfer.

Jim was injured while serving in Desert Storm and is now paraplegic. He practiced brace with Cody as described above. At first Jim was putting his hand on the top of Cody's head. This was very dangerous. Cody was a young, strong golden retriever who tried to please his owner and stiffened his neck muscles, but if Jim had continued working this way, it's likely that there would have been damage to Cody's neck or spine. As soon as Jim was made aware of the danger he moved his hand to Cody's shoulders and worked safely there. He began with light pressure on Cody's shoulders and built up gradually as he felt him stiffen against the pressure. This is how you build up your dog's muscles as well as his confidence.

Jim next practiced raising himself in his wheelchair, putting most of his weight on his hand on the rail of his chair and less weight on the hand braced on Cody. Soon he was able to use Cody's help to transfer from his chair. Once your dog has learned brace solidly you can experiment with different ways to use this command. Make sure he is solidly positioned before you lean on him, and make sure you put the weight on his shoulders.

CONCLUSION

You will need to decide the best ways to use your dog among all the possibilities this exercise offers. Remember that your dog must be large enough, physically strong enough, and in good health, or you should not even attempt any form of brace.

Don't hesitate to be inventive. You may come up with a perfect way to use your dog to help you that we never thought of. That's part of the teamwork. But always remember that you must put minimum weight on your dog, and always try to place that weight squarely on his shoulders to avoid the risk of injuring him. Please be careful. Any time you have any question about your dog's ability to do this exercise, consult your vet.

Even if all you're doing is lightly leaning on your dog for support, don't forget to praise him for being there. It may seem like a very small thing, and you may start to take it for granted, but your dog needs to hear your praise. That way he knows he's doing something that pleases you, and he will continue to do it to earn your praise.

Chapter 13

LIGHT
Teach your Dog to Turn a Touch Lamp On and Off

Sometimes there's a down side when your dog learns a new skill. Kim was working with her rottweiler, Xanth, to turn on a touch lamp. He enjoyed the practice because he was so liberally rewarded with praise and food. For the next several nights, Kim woke up each night to find the light turned up bright and Xanth sitting there proudly and expectantly.

When you come home at night to a dark house, it might be helpful to open the door and have your dog go in and turn on a light for you. After you're in bed you might want him to turn it off, and if you awaken during the night you might need the light back on.

Just about any dog of any size can be taught to turn lights on and off, as long as he can reach the lamp. We offer instruction on using the touch lamp because it is the neatest and easiest to teach a dog.

TOUCH LAMPS

A touch lamp is one that can be turned on simply by touching any metal part of the lamp. It usually has three brightness settings. Each time you touch it, it gets brighter, and on the fourth touch, it turns off. You can buy one at almost any store that sells lamps, or you can buy a device that screws into your current lamp and converts it to a touch lamp, if that lamp has a metal base. Touch lamps come in both floor and table models.

TEACHING TOUCH LAMP—MARY AND SAGE

Mary has had arthritis since she was two. It affects nearly every joint and her balance is precarious. If she comes home to a dark house, she might trip on something left on the floor. To prevent possible serious injury, Mary has taught each of her dogs to turn on a touch lamp.

Mary began by putting a touch lamp on a low table where her golden retriever, Sage, could reach it easily. She put a little piece of cheese on the metal base while Sage was watching. If you can't place the cheese (or other soft tempting treat), have a friend do it.

In a happy voice Mary said "light" and pointed to the cheese. Sage immediately licked the cheese off the base. As soon as her nose and tongue touched the metal, Mary exclaimed, "good light!" The light comes on, which acts as an additional reward.

At first, Sage had no idea what she did, but she liked it. This is an easy exercise to teach, because the reward is so automatic. Do it two or three times in a row. Make sure your dog doesn't get the cheese before you've given a command. He will get very eager as soon as he knows what's happening. You must keep him under control. Make him sit and stay as you place the cheese. If he moves toward the lamp before you tell him to, put him back in the stay. Then give your light command in a happy, playful voice. Use "easy" or "cool it" (see appendix) to settle him down if he's too excited. Make sure your dog hears the command "light" as he is touching the lamp.

Mary practiced for a week with cheese on the lamp every time. Sage

Teaching your dog to touch a lamp to turn it on or off is an easy but very useful exercise. Sedona (golden retriever)

was eagerly responding so Mary gave the command "light" without putting food on the lamp. Sage sniffed the base of the lamp for the treat and thus touched it and turned it on. Mary gave very enthusiastic praise and food treats from her hand.

When she tried again, Sage looked to her hand first. Mary simply pointed toward the lamp as she said "light." Sage followed her fingers, touched the lamp and received praise and food.

If your dog simply refuses to touch the lamp, he hasn't learned the word yet. Go back to step one and practice for another week with cheese on the base every time.

Mary worked at this level for at least a week with each of her dogs. Some dogs make the connection quickly that touching the lamp brings praise and a reward. Some dogs are so eager they keep touching with or without a command. Keep it under your control. He must touch it to your satisfaction, on your command, before he gets the praise and reward. Sometimes Mary would make her dog touch it more than once to raise the brightness level or to turn it off. Each touch brought praise and a repeat of the command. When the light was at the level Mary wanted, she praised, gave a food treat and moved away from the lamp.

Mary and Sage then backed a few feet away from the lamp. Mary put Sage on a stay and then put cheese on the base. She returned to Sage's side, pointed to the lamp and commanded "light." There was no hesitation because Sage saw the food.

Then Mary went through the same motions, except she did not actually put cheese on the base. When she gave the light command, Sage went right over to the lamp and touched the base. Mary gave very enthusiastic praise and Sage came to her for a food reward. If your dog doesn't touch the lamp without food on it, you need to go back to the beginning and practice longer with food every time. Make sure you give the light command as he touches the lamp.

Your goal is to be able to have your dog go over to the light by himself and turn it on. Any time he hesitates, point to the lamp and move toward it, if necessary. But he should go directly to the lamp. Practice from a few feet away for several days until you're sure that he is responding quickly and correctly to your command. Remember to praise every time and frequently give a food reward. Sometimes make him touch it again to raise the brightness level.

Mary then continued to move farther and farther away from the light, starting each step with cheese on the lamp as a reminder. Sage always got food as she began each step; then Mary would give it randomly. Don't stop food reward altogether. Occasionally, he should get a treat just to keep him on his toes. And always give appropriate praise.

PERFECTING LIGHT

Be careful to avoid static shocks. If it's winter and you're on carpet full of static electricity, your dog will get a shock as soon as his nose touches metal. Mary's first dog, a black terrier mix named Lucky, got one shock and refused to touch the lamp again. Most dogs aren't that sensitive. They frequently get a shock from us when we pet them but they keep coming back for more attention. If you keep the association positive and keep encouraging and rewarding your dog, he will accept an occasional shock.

If your dog is very exuberant, you might be worried that he'll knock the lamp right over in his eagerness to touch it and hurry back for a reward. To make it positive (and save the lamp) have a friend hold the lamp in the early stages. This will prevent it from crashing to the floor. Also use "easy" to calm him down. Work for a long time only a few steps away from the lamp so he learns the exercise in a more controlled manner.

Once your dog understands the concept of this command you can teach him to touch lamps anywhere in the house. He can learn to touch the base of a floor lamp as well as a table lamp. Start at step one with each new lamp, but you will progress very quickly, as long as he knows what the word means.

If your table lamp normally sits out of reach of your dog, you may have to teach him to put his paws gently up on the table to touch the lamp. (See chapter 5—Paws.)

If this is an exercise you rarely use, you will need to practice it occasionally to keep your dog sharp. If you use it frequently, don't forget to praise him when he does it. It's like saying "thank you." It's important to always praise desired behavior.

Chapter 14

PULL
Teach your Dog to Pull or Push your Wheelchair and to Pull a Cart

One of the first things Blake taught Savannah to do was to pull him in his wheelchair. The second thing he taught her was to stop. Next time he'll teach them in the reverse order! As they were flying down a sidewalk toward the curb with Blake yelling uselessly, "Stop! Halt! Hold it! Go back! Hellpp!" he envisioned himself doing his Superman impersonation. Or racing through a mall on the slick floor heading into a group of kids waiting for Santa, he envisioned trying to explain that Savannah was just a rampaging gold reindeer. Fortunately for all the times she wildly pulled him at breakneck speed, he never broke his neck (or anything else), and now she understands the concept of "slow down" and "stop." She doesn't like it as well as "pull," but she understands and obeys.

If your dog is strong enough there are many ways that you might use him to help you get around. He can learn to pull or push you in your manual wheelchair. He can pull you up out of a chair. He can also learn to pull a cart or laundry basket.

PULLING A WHEELCHAIR

If you want to train your dog to pull you in your wheelchair there are some things you must consider. Watch his position to make sure he is walking straight as he pulls you. If he walks at an angle leaning away he may do great damage to his shoulders or hips. How you hold the harness may affect the way he walks, so try to get a handle or strap that allows him to walk as straight as possible. Have a friend watch as you come toward him. If your friend tells you that your dog is straining, leaning or crossing over his front legs as he pulls you, try adjusting the way you hang on. Try a handle on the side of the harness instead of the top. If nothing seems to help, you should severely limit the times you ask him to pull you. Dogs enjoy moving out quickly; they enjoy pulling you along, so your dog will pull without complaint, even if it is slowly doing damage to his joints.

Your dog must be strong and in good physical condition to do this exercise. It's always a good idea to visit your vet. Tell him or her what you plan to teach your dog and get a thorough examination before you begin. Then be sure to build up slowly so your dog has a chance to get in shape.

He should wear a well-fitting harness designed for pulling. You can either grip the harness itself or attach a short leash to the harness and hold onto that. Or you might make a handle on the harness that's easy for you to grab.

Always start on a level surface with good footing for your dog. Find a quiet out-of-the-way place where you can practice without distractions. It might be helpful to bring along a friend.

TEACHING PULL—TODD AND MANNY

Todd is paraplegic as a result of a fall off a cliff. He is fairly athletic and uses a racing wheelchair, but sometimes he needs help from his lab mix, Manny. Todd worked with a friend the first few times, but once Manny understood what she was being asked to do, she enjoyed it immensely.

Todd began on a quiet neighborhood street that was paved and level. He made sure that the pavement wasn't too hot. Todd's friend, Anna, stood about six feet away holding some food treats. Todd took hold of Manny's harness, gave the heel command, and began rolling his chair forward. Anna showed the treats and called Manny, who immediately moved faster to reach Anna. As Manny felt resistance, Todd gave the command "pull" and Anna continued to entice her. Todd praised "good pull." Todd kept his right hand on the wheel to steer the chair straight and slow it down.

The first time they tried it, Manny was completely out of control trying to get to the food treats. As soon as she got to Anna she was leaping all around her. Todd realized he had to use the phrase "easy" (see appendix) to remind her to stay under control. It was also important that Todd be the one to give Manny the food reward.

They tried again with Anna about ten feet away. Manny had no trouble pulling, and Todd used his free hand to slow down the chair as he told her "easy." He praised "good pull." When they got to Anna, Todd commanded "halt" and then made Manny sit. He took the food from Anna and gave it to his dog.

They practiced this several times in a row over these short distances. The next day, when Todd was heeling over smooth terrain, he took hold of the harness and commanded "pull" as they kept rolling along. Todd kept pushing on the right wheel, which kept the resistance to a minimum. He praised Manny. She was learning to keep going forward even when she felt resistance, and she was being praised for it. She was learning the command "pull." At the same time, Todd was teaching her to move under control and to stop on his command.

When Todd felt that Manny understood the command, he and Anna worked with her on a slight incline. The resistance was much greater; Manny had to really pull in order to keep the wheelchair moving. Anna stood at the top of the ramp offering food and encouragement, and Todd helped by pushing the right wheel.

The first time, Manny stopped when she felt the weight of the chair. Todd went back down and this time got a running start on the level. He gave Manny the pull command before they started up the incline and Anna showed her the food reward waiting at the top. Todd encouraged her with "good pull," and their momentum carried them up the ramp. At the top, Anna gave the food treat to Todd to give to Manny.

Pulling on a level surface is easy and enjoyable for most dogs, and it may be very helpful to you, saving wear and tear on your shoulders and hands. Pulling up an incline may be more than your dog can do. You must decide how much he can handle. Don't ask him to pull too much weight or up too steep a hill. Remember that his muscles and joints must be sound for him to help you. It is up to you to see that he remains sound. If you see any sign of hesitation or lameness, take him to the vet.

Your dog can save wear and tear on your shoulders by pulling you in your wheelchair. Be sure he walks straight without straining. Blake Gigli (spinal cord injury T 12) and Bridgette (golden retriever)

TEACHING PUSH—LISA AND ROBERT

If you worry about your dog pulling you in your chair or if you don't have the strength to hold on while he pulls, you may be able to teach your dog to push your chair. This is probably better for a dog because he uses his shoulders and keeps his body straighter than when pulling. Many dogs have a natural tendency to go behind a wheelchair. Then they lower their heads to look through under the seat. This is the perfect position for pushing.

Lisa has Epstein-Barr virus disease, and was using a wheelchair most of the time when she was training her standard poodle, Robert. It was a strain on her hands and arms to maneuver her chair so she wanted him to learn to push her along when out in public. First she needed to teach him to go behind the chair.

Every time he came to her for attention, she would put her hand on the top of his head and push lightly. His natural tendency was to push back, and Lisa would say "good push." She has an excellent lilt to her voice when praising so Robert knew he was doing something that pleased her. To give him another clue Lisa began putting a glove on her hand and holding that as a target. He would push against her gloved hand and receive praise.

When he was consistently pushing against her hand held in front of him, Lisa began reaching her hand around behind her wheelchair. She would pat the back of the chair and encourage Robert to go behind and push on her hand. She gave enthusiastic praise each time he went back. At this time, there was no movement in her chair; she kept the brakes fully on. All she was teaching Robert now was to readily go behind her wheelchair on command and touch her hand at the back of the chair.

To begin teaching the actual push, Lisa set up on a level surface without obstacles. It's likely that you won't be able to go smoothly in a straight line when you first practice this. Your hands will be back and forth behind your chair and on your wheels, and your dog won't really know what's going on. Make sure you aren't going to crash into chairs or walls. You might want a friend present to help as needed.

Lisa put her gloved hand on the back of the chair and told Robert "behind" and "push." The brakes were off so the wheelchair moved forward when he pushed on her hand. This surprised him and he immediately came around to Lisa's side. She repeated the command and patted the back of the chair. He went behind and pushed again. Lisa gave enthusiastic praise as the chair moved forward. She used her other hand to keep the chair straight.

It usually only takes a time or two with enthusiastic praise for your dog to understand the concept. Most dogs find this an enjoyable experience. They get to move right out and they hear your happy praise. So the next important thing is to teach your dog to stop.

Lisa simply put increasing pressure on the wheels and told Robert "easy" and finally "stop." She praised him for the stop and had him come around to her side for a treat. Then she repeated the sequence. At first she only had Robert push for short distances so she could keep control while teaching him what was expected. It took time to make it a smooth operation. But he thoroughly enjoyed the experience. He went eagerly behind her chair and pushed with great enthusiasm. Every few feet he would stop pushing to look ahead, but went right back to the job with Lisa's encouragement. Lisa's task was to keep the chair straight and under control and watch for obstacles ahead.

Be aware of your dog's health and condition at all times. If he suddenly seems resistant to pushing you, get him to the vet. His muscles and joints must be sound for him to be able to help in this way. It might be a temporary problem requiring time to heal, or it might be a more serious condition that demands medical attention. You must be aware of your dog and respond to his needs.

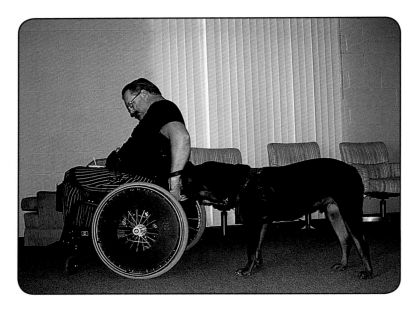

To teach your dog to push your chair, first teach him to go behind you on command. Fred Cook (spinal cord injury L 5) and Conrad (rottweiler)

PULLING A CART—SHERON AND SAM

If you want your dog to pull things for you in a cart you will need to find or design a lightweight cart that rolls easily.

Sheron was attending college and she needed to bring many things with her every day. Although complications from diabetes caused Sheron to be weak and visually impaired, she was determined to get her degree and go on to graduate school. Her Australian shepherd, Sam, provided great help by pulling a cart, which contained her books, notebooks, and computer.

Sheron began teaching Sam to pull the cart simply by getting him used to having it around. If your dog seems apprehensive of the cart, don't bring it too close to him. Simply leave it sitting in the room and praise your dog any time he goes near to investigate it. Place it near his feeding spot for a few days. Put some treats on the cart and give him permission to eat them. Move it around while talking to the cart and your dog in a happy voice.

Your dog must also get used to wearing a harness. This is usually no problem as long as the harness fits well. Sam wore his harness on walks and accepted it easily. Sheron then attached straps to rings on either side of the harness. She attached these straps to a lightweight plastic cart. She commanded Sam to heel and they moved out together. Sam was distracted at first by being followed, but Sheron encouraged him and praised as he heeled beside her.

Your dog must walk with you under excellent control before you try this. He must have confidence in your commands or he will be too disturbed by the cart to heel properly. Start slowly on a level surface. You don't want your dog to have to pull uphill, but even more important you don't want to go downhill where the cart may run into his legs. Praise enthusiastically and offer an occasional food reward.

You have to work as a team when your dog is pulling a cart. He will willingly haul your equipment, but will need your cooperation. Distribute items evenly within the cart so it's not heavier on one side and be sure items won't suddenly shift. Hold the side of the cart when going downhill to make sure it doesn't run him over. Design your cart so that it's easy for your dog to pull around and make sure he is strong enough and fit enough for what you need pulled. Visit your vet for a thorough exam before you try this.

SANDRA AND HOSS

Sandra has arthritis and wanted to teach her bouvier, Hoss, to pull a cart around the ranch. His temperament was a little more skittish than Sam's, so Sandra needed to build up in steps. She attached straps to rings on either side of the harness and then tied the straps to a small two-by-four board. She used food and lots of praise to encourage Hoss to heel beside her while dragging this strange object. The first time they only walked a few feet. Hoss was somewhat disturbed by the board trailing behind him.

Some dogs become very upset having something following them. If your dog is bothered, you want to take one step at a time. First just attach the straps to the harness and let him drag those around inside the house for short periods of time under your supervision. Praise and reward him with treats just for walking around. Don't praise him if he's showing fear. Use a happy voice and encourage him, but don't tell him it's okay to be afraid. It may take several sessions before he can relax with the straps dragging behind him.

When he's used to just the straps, wrap a small board in a towel and let him drag it around in the house. It's smoother and quieter inside until he gets used to the idea of having something following him. Then move outside. Keep encouraging him in a very happy manner.

Sandra and Hoss practiced three times the first day, with Hoss walking a few feet each time. Over the next several days she gradually built up the distance she asked Hoss to pull this light burden. He was getting used to

The cart that your dog pulls should be lightweight and roll easily. Sheron Neja (diabetes/neuropathy) and Sam (Australian shepherd)

A big strong dog, especially one bred for pulling, can be taught to pull heavier loads, as long as the cart rolls easily and the dog is properly conditioned. Sandra Schwartz (arthritis) and Hoss (bouvier des Flandres)

having something right behind him. If you build up slowly and positively, your dog should have no problem adjusting to this new situation.

Sandra next tied a metal pipe to the straps. She knew it would make more noise as it bounced on the ground, and she wanted Hoss to experience some of the noise a metal cart would make. He was uncomfortable the first few times they tried this, so she built up very slowly, going only a few feet each time with lots of praise, and then playing in the yard. Soon Hoss would pull the metal pipe all over the ranch.

Sandra then attached Hoss to the empty cart. He pulled it a few feet without difficulty because of all the preparations Sandra had taken. She praised enthusiastically and gave him a food reward. Slowly over the next several days Sandra added weight to the cart until Hoss was helping distribute hay and feed to the farm animals every day. Remember that slow is fast.

PULLING OTHER ITEMS

You can teach your dog to pull other items that may make things easier for you. You can put a strap on a laundry basket which you can clip to your dog's harness and teach him to pull it in the same manner as Sheron and Sandra taught pulling a cart. Or you can teach him to pull the basket by holding the strap in his mouth and walking with it. (See chapter 10—Retrieving and Carrying).

PULLING OUT OF A CHAIR—DIANE AND WHISKEY

If you want help getting up out of a chair, this is one method. See also chapter 12—Brace, where other methods are discussed. You can then decide which will work best for your needs.

Diane has arthritis and trained her golden retriever, Whiskey, to help her get up by actually pulling her out of the chair. Diane first got Whiskey used to wearing a harness. She simply put it on and let her wear it around the house for brief periods every day. After a few days Diane would occasionally tug on the harness as she said "pull, good pull." She did this for several days before she began the formal work.

Diane sat in a chair and taught Whiskey to sit in front of her facing away. Whiskey knew the sit command so Diane used food to show her the place she wanted her to sit.

Diane got her husband, Jerry, to help. She made sure that she felt well on the days she practiced this. During the learning stages it's important that you don't put too much strain on your dog or he'll balk at pulling. You need to help by being able to stand up easily as you teach what the word "pull" means. Diane sat in a chair and had Whiskey sit in front with Jerry standing a few feet away. Diane took hold of the harness. As she commanded "Whiskey, pull," Jerry called to her showing her a food treat. She immediately went toward Jerry, and Diane stood up, putting a minimum of strain on the harness. Whiskey felt the resistance but was concentrating on getting to Jerry so she pulled right through it. Diane praised enthusiastically and she took the treat from Jerry to give to Whiskey.

They practiced two or three times in a row every day for a week. Then Jerry stood nearby but didn't call to Whiskey or show a treat. Diane commanded "pull," and Whiskey immediately moved forward. Diane held onto the harness and let Whiskey's momentum actually pull her into the standing position. She gave enthusiastic praise and a food reward. Even with this added resistance Whiskey had learned what the word meant. If your dog hesitates when he feels the resistance, continue to use a friend to entice him forward. If you practice positively, your dog will soon understand that his job is to continue moving forward despite the increased pressure you put on the harness. You must praise for each small step forward.

CONCLUSION

More than most other exercises, pulling requires that you be very aware of your dog's physical condition at all times. You want this to be enjoyable as well as helpful and you certainly don't want to do lasting damage to his health. Seeing a dog flying along pulling his owner in a wheelchair is an awesome sight. Everyone's having fun, but it's your responsibility to make sure it's also safe. Your equipment must be of good quality and correct for the job. Your dog must be in good health. Build up gradually and positively, remembering that slow is fast. Even when your dog is consistently doing the exercises, he still needs to hear praise from you.

Your dog can learn to pull you up out of a chair and he can help you up stairs and ramps.
Diane Kounovsky (arthritis) and Whiskey (golden retriever)

Chapter 15

DRESS
Teach your Dog to Help you Get Dressed and Undressed

Beth will never know what possessed her to try on spandex leggings. They were bright and colorful and she just wanted to dress like everybody else. She knew she was in trouble as she struggled to get them on. They looked great but she realized that getting them off was going to be almost impossible because of her arthritis. If she hadn't had her retriever mix, Ollie, with her she might be wearing them to this day. It was a long and difficult struggle for Ollie to grip the slick fabric and pull. Amazingly, no one came in to check on them as Ollie kept sticking her rear end out the curtain and Beth kept repeating, "Ollie, pull! Ollie, back up!" An interminable 20 minutes later with both Beth and Ollie absolutely exhausted, Beth, with great dignity, turned the spandex leggings over to the clerk and said, "No, thank you, not today."

As amazing as it may sound, you can teach your dog to help you get dressed and undressed. It will depend on your particular needs whether you will find this exercise useful or not. Beth has rheumatoid arthritis, and sometimes her arms hurt too much at the end of the day for her to pull off her jeans. Her black lab/retriever mix, Ollie, learned to grab the cuff very gently and back up until Beth's leg was free.

Mary has juvenile rheumatoid arthritis. She is unable to bend all the way to the floor, so it was impossible for her to pull up a skirt or a pair of shorts. She taught her golden retriever, Sage, to take the material gently and lift it straight up until Mary could reach it.

Pam, also with arthritis, knew she had shoulder surgery coming up and it would be difficult for her to get her arms out of her shirt. She taught her German shepherd, Fallon, to take the sleeve and pull.

TEACHING DRESS

All of these examples show that your dog must have a solid take-it before he can be taught to help you either dress or undress. If your dog isn't taking things—anything you tell him to take—readily and consistently, you must work more on that command before you try this one. Practice with articles of your clothing—socks, shirts, pants. Make sure your dog takes them gently and brings them to you without trying to play with them. It could be dangerous to you if your dog displays too much enthusiasm in retrieving your clothes. Start with an old skirt or pair of shorts. It should be something that won't matter if it gets ripped.

When you have a solid take-it, decide where you need your dog's help the most. Then read the following examples of how these people taught their dogs. You may have to vary the methods, even devise your own way, but these methods will give you ideas.

GETTING DRESSED—MARY AND SAGE

Mary wanted to be able to pull on a skirt or a pair of shorts. She began with an old full skirt which she had Sage pick up off the floor and give to her several times. She used the command "take the dress," so she was combining the known command "take" with the new command "dress me." She used "easy" (see appendix) whenever Sage got too enthusiastic in her take-its. Mary gave praise every time, even after Sage was doing the exercise regularly. Food reward was used as an added incentive for each step.

Mary sat on the edge of a chair, laid the skirt on the floor and put her feet in the opening. She told Sage, "take the dress." If Sage tried to pull on it, Mary said "Uh-uh-uh" which Sage recognized as a correction, and then

You must teach your dog to raise the material straight up or he might pull you over.
Mary George (rheumatoid arthritis) and Sage (golden retriever)

"easy" to get Sage to handle the material gently. Mary praised enthusiastically when Sage lifted the skirt straight up. Thus Sage learned that there was a specific way to do "take the dress." She was corrected if she pulled away, and praised if she lifted straight up and gave it to Mary.

Next Mary tried the same thing while standing up. She dropped the skirt to the floor, stepped into the opening and told Sage "take the dress." Sage knew to lift the material up, but now she had to lift it higher to get it to Mary's hand. If Mary was stepping even a little bit on the material, Sage had to learn not to pull if she felt resistance. Again, Mary used "easy" to settle Sage down. Mary also had to use "wait" because Sage, in her enthusiasm, wanted to get the skirt as soon as Mary put it on the floor. She had to learn to wait until Mary had stepped into the opening and gave her the "dress" command.

Mary taught Sage to do the same thing with a pair of shorts. She began while sitting down, using a very baggy pair at first to make it easy for Sage to lift. In the beginning she only put one leg through the opening until Sage was reliably lifting the material up to Mary's hand in a gentle manner.

Then Mary stood up and got both feet into the proper openings. Again, Mary had to caution Sage to wait until she was ready—an eager dog will always try to anticipate what his owner wants. This needs to be handled gently and positively; you certainly don't want your dog to lose enthusiasm for the task. Use verbal corrections and signals that your dog already knows to keep him under control, but use enthusiastic praise and food to show him what you want. In time, your dog will be helping you pull on articles of clothing to make your life easier.

GETTING UNDRESSED—NORMA AND RANGER

For many people with disabilities, bending down to remove their socks can be a difficult task. With a little patience and perseverance, your dog can learn to do this for you. Just be sure you have plenty of old socks to work with.

Norma has neuropathy and lumbar fusion, and some days it's very hard for her to reach down and grab her socks to pull them off. Once her Belgian malinois mix, Ranger, was retrieving things without hesitation, Norma practiced with an old sock. She dropped it on the floor and said "take the sock." As soon as he picked it up, she praised "good sock," and said "give." He was used to picking things up and giving them to her so it was easy for him to do.

Next she laid the sock over her foot. She didn't put it on, just laid it on top and told Ranger to take the sock. He hesitated for a second because he wasn't sure about this location, but with encouragement, he took the sock and handed it to her. After several times doing it this way, Norma pulled the sock slightly onto her foot. Most of the sock was hanging off the end. She wiggled her foot as she commanded "take the sock." Ranger grabbed the end and it came off easily. Norma quickly commanded "give," so he didn't try to play with it like a toy.

They practiced at this level over several days. Norma kept it happy, but under control. If Ranger got too rambunctious in his eagerness to take the sock, Norma would tell him "easy" which helped to settle him down. Then Norma pulled the sock farther onto her foot. Only a little extra sock was hanging over the end of her toes. Now it was especially important that Ranger do this command under control. It's easy for your dog to nip your toes in his enthusiasm.

Also now he will have to actually pull at the sock to make it come off. It's no longer a simple matter of taking the item. Ranger felt resistance and immediately dropped the sock. Norma had to encourage him to take it again and again. Then she commanded "back" (see chapter 8—Reverse). This was a command he knew, but now it was in combination with another command, and Norma had to be patient for him to understand that he needed to take the sock, hold onto it, and back up.

The first time he did it and the sock came off her foot, Norma gave enthusiastic praise and a jackpot of treats. This told Ranger that he had done something wonderful. The only problem was that he took her excitement as an invitation to play and he ran around with the sock in his mouth! She calmly told him to bring it to her and give, and she praised quietly when he did. You have to find the happy medium between enough enthusiasm to keep him interested and enough calm to keep him under control.

As they practiced, Norma moved the sock farther and farther up on her foot until it was all the way on. Ranger had to learn to grab the object without grabbing the toes underneath. Norma would yelp if he pinched her toes and tell him "easy." Then tell him to take the sock again. He soon learned what was expected. Norma always helps him by using her other foot to push the sock down to her heel so it's easier for him to pull it off. But even with tight socks, he will take hold of it and pull until it comes off. Then he gives it right to her and goes for the other one.

GETTING UNDRESSED—BETH AND OLLIE

Some days it's impossible for Beth to remove her jeans at the end of the day. She ended up sleeping in them more than once because it was simply too painful. She decided her retriever mix, Ollie, could learn to help.

Beth began by teaching Ollie to take a sock, just as Norma taught Ranger. Socks are easy to work with and cheaper to replace than pants. She worked up to Ollie having to back up to pull the sock off. She would really need to do that to help remove a pair of pants. Ollie quickly learned that if there was any resistance she had to pull and back straight up in order to release the sock from Beth's foot.

Next, Beth cut a section of leg material off an old pair of jeans and draped it over her leg. Going back to the beginning steps of take-it, they quickly worked up to Beth pulling this onto her leg beyond her foot. This is where Ollie really had to learn.

First, Beth had to teach her to always take the material from the bottom, from under Beth's heel. If Ollie tried to take the top, there was no way to pull it over the foot; she had to come from underneath. Beth would hold her leg up and point to the proper place while she encouraged take-it. If Ollie reached for the wrong place, Beth would correct with a gentle "no-no" or "uh-uh-uh" and keep showing her the right place to grab. She praised happily each time Ollie took hold under the heel.

Teach your dog to take the material gently and then pull away. With socks, he'll have to learn to watch out for your toes. And with pants, he must grip the pant leg under the heel and pull straight back. Top—Norma Mckee (neuropathy, lumbar fusion L 4-5 & L 5-S 1) and Ranger (Belgian malinois mix) Bottom—Beth Harris (rheumatoid arthritis) and Ollie (retriever mix)

Even when Ollie gripped the material in the correct spot, she encountered real resistance trying to get it over Beth's heel. Many times Ollie showed confusion and frustration, but Beth would patiently go back one step so that Ollie could succeed. Beth would pull the material just over her heel and Ollie would take it and pull it off. Eventually Ollie realized she just needed to persist. The first time that Ollie got the material over Beth's heel, Beth gave her very enthusiastic praise and a big jackpot of treats. This gave Ollie the encouragement to succeed the next time as well.

Beth had to keep reminding Ollie of the command "back." Ollie would pull the material over Beth's foot and then assume the exercise was over. Beth had to patiently repeat "take jeans" and "back up." Taking off a pair of pants requires your dog to back up quite a distance. Ollie persisted because of Beth's encouragement but she found it very tedious and never liked doing this exercise. Beth had to be very patient each time Ollie quit and came for her reward before the exercise was finished.

You must show patience and understanding as your dog struggles to learn something new, especially something this complex and laborious. Always be willing to back up a step or two to the level where your dog can succeed and work at that level until you see that he has confidence. Work with him as a team to make this successful. For instance, you'll have to get your pants down off your hips before he can be expected to pull them the rest of the way off. Remember to praise with enthusiasm each time he masters the smallest of steps, and your corrections should be few and very gentle.

GETTING UNDRESSED—PAM AND FALLON

Arthritis made taking off a shirt or jacket difficult and sometimes painful for Pam. Upcoming shoulder surgery would help in the long run but during rehabilitation she knew she'd need help from her German shepherd, Fallon.

Pam cut a loose sleeve off an old shirt and began just laying it across her arm. She taught Fallon to take this piece of material gently. Then she put her hand just inside the loose sleeve and trained Fallon to pull it off. Next she held the material with her other hand to give it some resistance. Using the command "sleeve" she kept encouraging Fallon to pull the material. She had to use the phrase "easy" repeatedly to keep Fallon from pulling too hard too quickly and ripping the sleeve.

Pam let the material slide off her arm, easily at first, then with increasing resistance by holding it with her other hand. Fallon learned to persist in pulling, but to do it in a controlled manner, working with her owner. You may want to teach your dog to back up (see chapter 8—Reverse)

You must train your dog to grip the sleeve gently and you must help get it over your shoulder and elbow. Sandra Schwartz (arthritis) and Chance (bouvier des Flanders)

and use that command so that he pulls straight back with the material in his mouth.

When they tried a real sleeve for the first time, Pam first got it over her shoulder. It was a very loose sleeve so that as Pam moved her arm, it came easily over her elbow and off. Pam and Fallon learned how to work together as a team to make this possible. Fallon could never simply pull on a sleeve without ripping it unless Pam cooperated to get it over her shoulder and elbow.

In time, following patient practice and using teamwork, Fallon was able to help with almost any shirt or jacket or coat. Pam doesn't ask for her help with thin silk material or very tight shirts. It would be difficult for Fallon to get them off without ripping them. Use common sense in what you ask your dog to do and be understanding if something gets torn in the process. Work with dispensable clothes until you are sure that your dog knows what to do and does it under control.

CONCLUSION

There are many ways you may be able to use your dog's help in getting clothes on and off. The basic technique is to work slowly, positively, and creatively with your dog. Once you have a solid take-it, it's just a matter of teaching him what to do with the object he's taken. Think about what help your dog can provide in assisting you getting dressed and undressed. Don't hesitate to be creative, and remember that slow is fast.

Be very aware of your own health when teaching this exercise. If you're in pain don't practice this because the slightest touch to an inflamed joint could cause you to yell in agony. Your dog will assume that he has done something wrong which will set back the training. Don't hesitate to use the various self-help devices available until your pain is under control.

Chapter 16

DOORS
Teach your Dog to Help you Open and Close Doors

Claudia taught her dog, Joda, to open doors for her wherever they went. Joda was a typical border collie who took jobs very seriously. So one day when they went to the mall, Joda was about to pull open the door when a man came up and graciously held the door for Claudia. Joda was visibly upset to have this task taken away; even the kind stranger could see his disappointment. Claudia explained how important work was to Joda, so the man let the door shut. Joda happily pulled it open for his owner to go through, and then held it for the man too.

If you have trouble opening and closing doors, your dog can learn to assist you. You will need to take into consideration how heavy the door is and how big and strong your dog is. Depending on the doors you encounter routinely, you may have to teach your dog two or three separate exercises. Remember: to you it's opening a door; to your dog it's performing a sequence of exercises that you teach him and for which he's rewarded. He doesn't know that pushing the button on the automatic door and pulling on a strap on the manual door are the same thing. You must look at all the parts of each exercise and thoroughly teach them to your dog.

PUSHING A BUTTON—STEWART AND LAURA

This is probably the easiest way for your dog to learn to open doors for you. If you go to a mall where there's a choice between an entrance with a heavy glass door that you open manually or one with an automatic opening door, you would be wise to go through the automatic door. It's easier on both of you.

Because Stewart had cerebral palsy, it wasn't possible for him to hold a treat. In this exercise you need the treat held in a specific place (on or near the button) to focus your dog's attention on that location. So don't hesitate to enlist a friend to help if you can't hold the treat up near the button.

Stewart and his friend, Zenona, went to the mall early in the day so there would be few distractions. It won't help your training if people keep trying to be helpful and open the door for you. Stewart sat his yellow lab, Laura, about a foot away from the button. Zenona held a small treat in front of Laura and then moved it slowly away and up above the button. As Laura moved forward to follow the treat, Stewart said "button," and praised and encouraged her. As the treat was raised above the button, Stewart said "lap," a command Laura already knew. (See chapter 5—Paws). She put her front feet up in response to both the command and the position of the treat, and her paws touched the button. Stewart gave enthusiastic praise. Zenona put the treat on Stewart's lap and he gave Laura permission to have it.

This sounds more complicated than it is. You need to remember that the commands, praise, and ultimately the food reward must all come from you. Coach your friend on how he or she can help, but make sure that you are in charge of all aspects of the training. At this point, your dog will have no idea what he did, but praise with enthusiasm anyway.

Stewart practiced twice more. Each time Laura followed the treat and obeyed the lap command. Since the button sticks out, it was natural that she rested her front paws there. The third time they tried it, she went up quickly and enthusiastically so that her feet pushed hard enough to open the door.

Placing food on or above the button will cause your dog to reach up to get it. When he puts his paw on the button, the door will open and you can praise. Soon he will push the button on your command. Laura (yellow lab)

Stewart was wild in his praise and had Zenona put three treats on his lap for Laura. Laura was not startled by the door opening, but be aware that your dog might be. Continue to praise in an excited manner so he realizes that this is a positive thing.

They walked around the mall for a few minutes before going back to the button. This time Stewart had Zenona hold the treat directly above the button. Stewart combined the commands "lap, button," and Laura got right up on her hind legs, again accidentally pushing the button with her front feet. Stewart praised enthusiastically and Zenona placed the treat on his lap where he gave Laura permission to take it. Laura still had no idea what she had done, but she was happy to receive the praise and food reward. They did the sequence two more times with a treat being held just above the button.

They came back the next day and repeated the exercise. The first time, Stewart used the combined command. Then he dropped "lap" and just used "button." Laura soon came to understand that what brought the reward was putting her paw on the button.

After a week of practice Stewart moved back three feet from the button. Zenona held the treat above it and Stewart told Laura "button." She immediately went over and put her paws up, pushing the button. Stewart praised as Zenona brought the treat back and put it on Stewart's lap.

Then Stewart gave the command without Zenona holding a treat above the button. Laura hesitated for a second and Stewart repeated the command in an encouraging way. Laura went toward the button but hesitated again. So Stewart moved forward pointing to the button. Laura put her front paws up and received lavish praise and a jackpot of treats from Stewart's lap.

Stewart practiced on different buttons inside and outside the mall. To Laura each was a new exercise, but it took only a few minutes to teach her to press each new one. Sometimes noise reverberates inside a mall so much that your dog may find it more difficult to listen and obey you. Be patient. Work with praise and food until your dog is confident. Continue to give a treat occasionally, and always give verbal praise.

If the button is within reach of your dog's head, you might teach him to push it with his nose or forehead instead of his paw. To push it with his nose, use a treat such as cheese that you can actually stick on the center of the button and praise enthusiastically when your dog licks it off. To use his head, see in chapter 14 the section on learning to push a wheelchair. Use the same basic techniques and transfer the push from your hand to the door button. If the button seems too stiff for him to press easily, teach him to use his paw.

OPEN DOORS BY PULLING A STRAP—CHRIS AND KOA

Your dog must have a reliable take-it before you can begin this exercise. If you have a door at home that you want your dog to open, you can tie a leather strap or old belt to the handle and leave it there. Remember that once your dog learns how to open the door he can do it whenever he wants. If you think this might be dangerous, then don't leave the strap on, or make sure the door is locked except when you want him to open it.

There is a lever that you can buy that fits over a regular doorknob. It may make it easier for you to open your door, and it's the easiest way to teach your dog to help. This handle is sold by the Arthritis Foundation. Many different kinds of handles are also available from other self-help groups. You can also replace the regular doorknob with French door handles.

You can tie a piece of cord or leather strap to this handle, but it might slip off while your dog is tugging on it, so it's probably best to drill a hole near the end of the handle and put the strap through. To the other end of the strap you can attach something for your dog to take, such as a ball or toy or nylabone. Again, you can tie them to the strap or for more permanence you can drill a hole and put the strap through. The strap should be short so that your dog has to reach up to grab it. This will force him to pull down, which will depress the handle.

Chris injured his spinal cord in a diving accident in Hawaii. Because of limited arm movement and strength, it's difficult for him to open doors. His eager Australian shepherd, Koa, was easy to train and Chris was able to teach him several different ways to open and close doors. Chris also devised a strap with Velcro to attach to a doorknob and slip over the handle. You can see this on the Teamwork II DVD.

Before he attached the strap to the door handle, Chris practiced several take-its with the strap until Koa was readily taking it. Then he put it on the handle. He told Koa to take it and praised when Koa just looked at the strap. He repeated the take command until he grabbed it. Then Chris praised with enthusiasm and gave him a treat. This strap is now in a strange location and your dog may hesitate, unsure of what he's supposed to do. Touch the strap if possible and keep encouraging him. He will usually readily take a ball or a toy on the end of the strap.

Chris practiced two or three times in a row using lots of enthusiastic praise and giving a treat each time Koa took the strap. Then he moved away and played some fetch. Several hours later, they tried again. Koa was a quick study so Chris began to combine it with the second part of this exercise—backing up. See chapter 8—Reverse, and teach your dog a reverse command separately from this door command. He must understand the concept of backing up.

Position yourself where the door will hit you before it opens too far too quickly and hits your dog, or have a friend stand by to catch the door. Chris told Koa "take" and praised quietly as soon as he grabbed the strap. He told Koa to hold it and then commanded "back." If your dog drops it, tell him to take it again and be sure to say "hold," and then command "back." It may take several tries before your dog realizes that he has to keep hold of the strap as he obeys your reverse command.

Koa backed up with the strap still in his mouth, so the door swung open. Koa was startled and dropped the strap, but Chris praised him enthusiastically and gave him a treat. Chris stopped the momentum of the door with his wheelchair and then pushed it closed. He repeated the sequence. Koa hesitated to take the strap but Chris kept encouraging him. Be patient. The opening of the door is something strange, and your dog may be confused by the events. With encouragement, Koa took the strap and backed up, opening the door. Again, he received praise and a treat, so he decided this was a good thing.

Once your dog has a solid take-it, he can be taught to pull a strap to open or close doors for you. Zio (labradoodle)

Your dog can learn to pull even a heavy gate and will then open or close it on your command. Tasha (rottweiler/shepherd)

Be sure that you or your friend catches the door before it hits your dog. You don't want him to become afraid of it. Practice regularly with lots of praise.

SANDY AND TASHA

Sandy had Behcets and fibromyalgia which sometimes made it difficult for her to do her chores—taking care of her horses, chickens and other animals. Her shepherd/rottweiler mix, Tasha, was a big help, opening and closing the gate on the ranch. Sandy tied a rope to the gate and taught Tasha to take the rope and walk with it in her mouth. The gate was large and it took a good strong pull to get it started. Then it would move easily. Tasha had to learn to stay out of its way as she pulled on the rope. Sandy praised for each small step and was generous with food reward in the early stages of training. Tasha frequently dropped the rope, and Sandy had to patiently encourage her to take it again and continue pulling. Once she learned what was expected, she was happy to grab the rope whenever Sandy told her to and pull the gate until it was either open or closed.

Remember to be liberal with praise and food as you teach this exercise, then give a treat occasionally. Always praise each time your dog opens the door on your command. Remember that he now knows how to open the door and may do it on his own. Be very careful that this doesn't create a dangerous situation.

OPEN DOORS WITH PAWS—CHRIS AND KOA

Learning to pull on a strap in the manner described above is for doors that open toward you. For a door that opens away from you, your dog can easily learn to push down on the handle with his paws and push it open. You need the same type of handle over the doorknob, something for the dog to push down on.

Chris wanted Koa's help both in pulling open doors and pushing them open. He had Koa on a short leash next to his wheelchair. When Chris faced the door, Koa was right below the handle. Chris said "paws" and pointed toward the door. (See chapter 5—Paws). As Koa raised his front paws up, Chris praised "good paws" and then said "door."

Koa's paws automatically hit the handle and Chris praised with great enthusiasm—"good door." As the handle was depressed, Koa's weight naturally pushed the door open. Chris praised again and gave Koa a treat. Although Koa really had no idea what he'd done, he knew it pleased Chris so he was anxious to repeat it.

Chris had a friend close the door and tried it again. Koa missed the handle

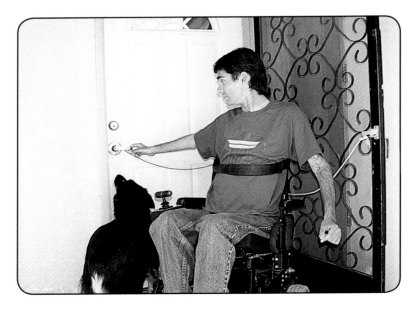

When teaching your dog to push down a door handle with his paws, position yourself so that your dog is directly under the handle. Chris Wenner (spinal cord injury C 5-6) and Koa (Australian shepherd)

this time when he put his paws on the door, so nothing happened. Chris praised for the paws, then told Koa "off." He moved his wheelchair so that Koa was positioned right under the handle. When he said, "paws, door" Koa put his feet on the handle. It pushed easily and the door again opened. Chris praised enthusiastically and gave him a treat.

It only took three or four repetitions before Koa understood that "door" meant to put his paws on the handle and push. It may take longer for your dog, but keep practicing and he will get the idea. Make sure you set up for success each time in the beginning so he doesn't have to think about what to do. When he gets the idea of what the command word means, you can be several feet away from the door and tell him to open it, and he will.

Remember to put a command word to the action and choose the word carefully. To you, having him pull the strap to open the front door and push the handle to open the back door are the same thing. He's opening a door. But to your dog, they are very different actions. So use different commands. And remember to praise when he does it.

If your dog tries to open the door on his own, give him a correction, such as "uh-uh-uh or "no door." This should be something he does only on your command.

CLOSING DOORS—HELEN AND FLUTTER

Flutter is a cute little papillion who helps her owner, Helen, around the house by picking up small objects. There are a lot of things small dogs can't do, but one thing Helen wanted from Flutter was for her to close the door. She will leave the door open so her three little dogs can go in and out at will. But if it becomes too cold or starts to get dark, Helen wants the door closed. With her arthritis, it was sometimes painful to have to get up and go over to close the door. Her door swings easily so she knew it wouldn't be difficult for Flutter to push her paws against it and have it close.

She began by teaching Flutter the "lap" command. (See chapter 5—Paws). To transfer this to the door, Helen decided to use the clicker method. She felt that she was sometimes inconsistent in using the same command word every time, so she thought the clicker would bring consistency into the training process. She stood close to the door, which was shut, and held the treat right on the door just out of reach. Hearing the paws up command, Flutter reached for the treat and put her paws against the door. Helen clicked the clicker, praised with enthusiasm and gave her the treat. She practiced this several times. To teach your dog this specific exercise, start with a compound command. Say, "paws, door," putting emphasis on the word "door." After a few times, you can drop the word "paws."

At first, Flutter didn't put her paws up high enough so Helen raised the treat up the door, encouraging Flutter to reach for it. When she was in the right position, Helen would click and treat.

After practicing two or three times a day for a week, Helen stood a few feet from the door and gave the command. Flutter was confused and put her paws on Helen's leg. Helen gave a gentle verbal correction and took a step toward the door, repeating the command. She held the treat out close to the door. Finally Flutter put her paws on the door and Helen gave very enthusiastic praise and gave her several treats. It took Flutter several days of practice to begin to get the idea of going right to the door when she heard the command. She would often hesitate and stay near Helen because she had the treat. But in time Flutter learned that the way to get the treat was to go to the door and put her paws up. Then she would hear the clicker, signaling good job.

All this time the door had been closed. Once Flutter was regularly going to the door and putting her paws on it, Helen opened the door a few inches and stood right next to it. She gave the command and Flutter put her paws up. The door moved, which startled her. But Helen clicked the clicker and gave excited praise, telling her that this was exactly what she wanted. They did it again right away, and this time Flutter seemed to expect the door

Your dog can learn to push on the door to close it for you.
Helen Leavenworth (rheumatoid arthritis) and Flutter (papillon)

to move. Sometimes, because Flutter does everything so fast, she would barely touch the door and jump back for her treat. So Helen held the treat on the door for a few seconds, delaying the click and the treat long enough for Flutter to get a good push.

It was now just a matter of building up distance away from the door. Helen took it very slowly moving only a foot or two farther each time. If Flutter seemed confused, Helen went back beside the door and worked there a time or two to remind her what she was supposed to do. There was always lots of praise and encouragement. Eventually, Helen reached the point where she could sit in her chair and command "door." Flutter would race across the room, push the door with flair, and run back to Helen for praise and an occasional treat.

You might have to add an additional command to this. If Flutter is too quick rushing to the door and back for her praise and treat, she sometimes doesn't push hard enough to close it. Helen added "harder" and Flutter learned to go back and push it again. Jane's labradoodle, Zio, pulls her screen door closed with a strap, but occasionally it doesn't latch. Jane commands "slam it," and Zio will pull again, with more force.

HOLDING A DOOR OPEN—KELLIE AND ATLEE

Kellie was ten years old when she began training her German shepherd, Atlee. She has juvenile rheumatoid arthritis and was quite small at that time. The screen door to her house was a heavy metal door on a spring. If Kellie's mom was not home to hold the door for her, it was difficult for Kellie to brace the screen while she unlocked the front door. She worked out a method whereby Atlee could provide the help she needed.

Kellie had already taught Atlee to sit in various places and to stay sitting for different lengths of time. When this was solid, Kellie and her mother, Patti, worked with Atlee at the front door. They opened the screen door all the way with Patti holding it open. Kellie commanded Atlee to sit and stay in the opening, facing away from the door. Kellie then commanded "door" as Patti closed the screen door slowly until it just touched Atlee. Be sure your dog's tail will not be pinched when the door touches him. Teach a "tuck your tail" command if it seems to be a problem (see appendix), or teach your dog to sit sideways to the door so his tail is out of the way.

Kellie commanded "stay, door" as the door touched her dog, and praised her for remaining seated. Patti never let go of the door; she held it so it was just lightly touching Atlee. After a few seconds Kellie praised Atlee and released her. They walked around and then came back to the door.

Kellie put Atlee in position in the door opening and Patti let the screen door rest a little more heavily against Atlee's hip. Kellie repeated her "door, stay" command and praised "good door." They practiced this several times over the next few days with Patti allowing more and more of the door's weight to rest against Atlee. They also built up the time that Atlee was required to hold the door. If your dog moves away from the pressure, go back to the beginning, then build up slowly.

Atlee got used to the feel of the door against her and she consistently remained in her sit stay despite the pressure of the door. Then Patti stood aside while Kellie and Atlee tried to do it for themselves.

She opened the heavy screen door and then placed Atlee on a sit stay in the opening. As she commanded "door," she carefully allowed the door to close until it was leaning on Atlee. Be careful not to let the door close too quickly or too hard against your dog. It's your responsibility to make sure the closing door won't hurt him; he's trusting you by remaining in the sit stay. Patti was standing close enough to grab the door if necessary.

Kellie praised Atlee and repeated "door, stay." She then opened the front door. As she did, she praised again, reminding Atlee that she was still on command. It was important that Atlee not move yet or the screen door might have knocked Kellie over. Once the front door was opened, Kellie

Teaching your dog to hold open a door must be a team effort. Kellie makes sure the door rests gently against Atlee; then, after Kellie is in, she holds the door for Atlee.

turned around and held the screen door. She then released Atlee from the stay, telling her to go in the house. This kept the door from bumping Atlee as she got up. After they were both in the house, Kellie rewarded Atlee with a hug and a food treat.

They continued to practice until Atlee was solid. This was an especially helpful part of Kellie's daily routine. Atlee held the screen door for Kellie; then Kellie held it for Atlee. They both got in without difficulty and without needing Mom to open the door.

DOORS IN PUBLIC

It can be very difficult to train a dog to open the heavy glass door in most public places. That's why we encourage you to use automatic doors whenever possible. If there are some doors you would like to teach your dog to open, you might want to work with a local trainer to come up with the best way to make it work. There may be some devices that you can place over the handle and teach your dog to pull, but then it's difficult to retrieve the device, and you will have to work with your dog to brace the door open so he can come through. It can be done, but it will take patience, ingenuity, and time.

Chapter 17

YOU'RE STILL NOT FINISHED

Mary and Kevin had been dating for several months when he began acting strangely. He finally confessed that he was a little jealous of Mary's golden retriever, Sage. Everywhere they went, people greeted Sage before they even looked at Kevin. Because they cared deeply for each other, they were able to talk it through and Mary became more conscious of introducing Kevin to her friends before they made a fuss over Sage. By the time their wedding came around, Kevin was thrilled to have Sage carry a basket of flowers down the aisle. And when Mary said she had arranged for Lydia to take Sage home right after the wedding, Kevin exclaimed, "What? She's not coming on the honeymoon?"

At the end of Teamwork we wrote that your work with your dog was not done, whether you wanted to continue on and teach service exercises or not. You took the challenge to move on to the next level and now you have a dog who is not only a good companion but a helpmate as well. You've worked hard to achieve this. We told you in book one that training your dog in basic obedience was something most people never accomplish. Having a service dog is even rarer. Well, your work still isn't done.

CERTIFICATION

At this time there are few standards for service dogs. The ADA simply says that a disabled person cannot be separated from his service dog. Though this certainly may change in the future, at this time, no level of training is required; no test is necessary; no license is issued.

This puts the responsibility squarely on you. If you plan to take your dog in public, you should only be satisfied if his training is superior and his control is excellent. You should know that you have his attention no matter the distractions; you should know that he is trustworthy around adults, children and dogs; you should know that he is confident and friendly and happy to be with you; you should know that he is healthy and well-groomed.

TOP DOG offers certification for people who have trained their own dogs. To achieve this you must go through the certification test that is given to students who complete the TOP DOG program. The advantage is having identification that you can show if you are ever denied admittance to a public facility. It validates the work you've done. It says to the world that you and your dog are a qualified TOP DOG team.

If you're interested in finding out about certification, visit our website at topdogusa.org or contact us at the address in the front of the book.

CONTINUING EDUCATION

You have invested a lot of time and energy training your dog to this level. We hope it's been fun for both of you and thus you will have no problem continuing your work. Your dog will lose any exercise that you don't practice regularly. If you haven't had him go under a table for months don't be surprised if he doesn't instantly obey you in a crowded restaurant. Be patient and remember your first steps in training the exercise. He will remember and obey as soon as you make it clear. Continue to practice all the skills you've taught him to keep him sharp. You never know when you may need his prompt obedience.

Don't hesitate to try a new skill. Your needs may change or you may just want to keep your dog attentive by teaching him something new. That's the advantage of learning to do the training yourself; you have the skill to figure out how to teach a brand new exercise. It's good for both of you. No matter how old he is or how long it's been since you were actively schooling him he can continue to learn as long as you teach in a patient and positive manner. You can teach tricks, like shake hands, high five, roll over, or take a bow. It will amaze your friends and keep an enjoyable working relationship going between you and your dog.

Remember to praise your dog for his correct responses and continue to give him an occasional treat as a reward. Praise keeps both of you relaxed and cheerful and makes you a better and happier team. It's something that you want to be conscious of doing for your dog's whole life. You can cut way back on the food rewards. An occasional treat is like a Christmas bonus, but it should certainly happen more than once a year.

CHANGES

Our lives change; that's a fact. You may get married or divorced. You may have children. You may go back to work or school. You may move.

All of these events will have a profound effect on your dog as well as on you. It's easy to forget him in all the confusion, but this is when he needs you more than ever. Spend as much time as possible with him. Try to stick to his normal routine as much as you can. If you've been taking him everywhere with you and now you leave him home alone for hours at a time, don't be surprised if he reverts to puppy behavior—chewing, barking, digging. Things that he doesn't understand are swirling around him and he's looking for a way to cope. Be patient and understanding. Do everything you can to ease these transitions for him.

On the other hand, if you haven't taken your dog in public very much and now you want to bring him along to school or to work, don't just plunge in. Reread chapter 4—In Public—to help you prepare, and build up slowly so you both gain confidence.

If a new person is added to the household—either a spouse or a child—your dog will feel the changes as much as or more than you do. He will experience an emotion similar to jealousy unless you include him in the events. Dogs have the capacity to share their devotion with several people. If your spouse spends some quality time interacting with your dog it will be an easy transition. You should still maintain leadership but your dog can learn to love and obey your spouse as well.

If you're having a baby, it's important that you make your dog a part of it. It's very easy to ignore him because of all the demands of parenthood, but it's critical that he be included. Supervise his interactions with the baby

Changes are part of life. When a baby is added to your family, it's important to include your dog as much as possible, but supervise their interactions. Barry Butler (spinal muscular atrophy) and Taffy (samoyed/Australian shepherd) with Anna, 6-week old Rebekah and 3-year old Jeremiah

As your dog grows older, take his needs into consideration. Limit the physical tasks you ask him to perform. But keep him fit and active. Blake Gigli (spinal cord injury T 12) and Bridgette (golden retriever)

and lavish praise on him so he doesn't see the baby as something negative. Also watch the baby's actions around your dog. Babies tend to grab and pull, and your dog's ears and tail are easy targets. If introduced in a positive manner and supervised attentively, dogs and children make wonderful companions.

Divorce is a very emotional time for everyone involved. Your dog will recognize how deeply emotional everybody has become, but he won't be able to understand what's happening. Just as you would protect and help a small child through these times, you must be equally considerate of your dog. Try to keep to his routine as much as possible. It will help you deal with the difficult times to spend time with your dog. He will be loving and non-judgmental through it all.

You have a responsibility throughout all these changes to remember how much your dog has done for you and how much he needs you. Don't let him get lost in the shuffle.

OLDER DOG

As your dog grows older you will notice changes both physically and mentally. Some changes are so gradual you will hardly be aware of them until you suddenly realize that he's sleeping more often and more soundly. He doesn't hear you pick up your keys or the dog cookie box. He gets up and walks more slowly.

These are all normal changes. You need to be alert and respond appropriately. First of all you should take him to the vet more frequently, at least once a year. Consult with your vet on specific geriatric considerations— diet, exercise, medical checks. Older dogs need a food appropriate for their age. They need moderate exercise to keep them as limber as possible while taking into consideration arthritis or hip problems. It's important that your older dog not be overweight as this is very hard on his joints.

If your dog develops arthritis you will need to modify your demands on him. He may not be able to lift or carry heavy objects. If he normally laps to give you an item, you might have to devise another method. Some days will be worse than others and you will have to be especially considerate of him on bad days. He may not be able to jump into the car or walk around the block. Helping you up or pulling your wheelchair will be too much for him.

As hard as it is to think about, your wonderful, faithful companion and friend will age. Ultimately you will probably have to come to a decision about when to let him go. No one can make this decision for you; only you will know when the time is right. The final gift we can give to our dogs is to let them die with dignity. But it's a very difficult time. You have a right to grieve. You will have lost a member of your family. Try to focus on the positive memories, all the good times and all the ways your dog was a helper and friend. The love that you shared will always stay alive between you.

A NEW DOG?

As your dog gets older and more frail, you may start to consider when to acquire and train a new dog. Should you get the new one before or after your current dog dies? Is it a betrayal to bring in another dog?

Your personal circumstances will answer those questions. If you have space for two dogs and the capacity to care for a second dog, you may find it very helpful to bring in a new dog before your current friend is too old. In many ways your older dog will help you train your new one. He may not be happy at first with the intrusion, but if you ease him into the situation it usually works well. You must continue to spend quality time with your older dog. Don't stop working with him and concentrate all your attention on the newcomer. Slowly transfer various jobs to the younger dog while making sure you reserve some skills specifically for your old pal. Many older dogs actually seem to act younger having a young dog around, like a second childhood. But be aware that your current service dog might revert to adolescent behavior as a response to the newcomer—chewing, going to the bathroom in the house or barking. If it happens, this is usually a temporary situation. Simply go back to the basics for a few days to re-establish your leadership.

If circumstances don't allow a second dog, then be prepared for a period of time without canine help. One important thing to remember is that you put a lot of work into training your dog—he didn't come that way. Don't compare the new dog to the old. They are totally different animals, even if they're the same breed, even if they're related. How you work with the youngster may be very different from all your previous experience. Give him a chance to be himself. Go back to the book Teamwork to remember how to teach the basics. This will help you remember all the fun and all the frustrations you had as you began training. Enjoy the experience all over again. You have learned to be an observer of your dog and have acquired basic teaching skills. This time around might be easier.

CONCLUSION

We hope that you have enjoyed the experience of training your dog and continue to practice all exercises and even teach new skills. If you have questions or comments, you can contact us through TOP DOG Publishing. We would love to hear from you.

You and your dog have achieved something accomplished by very few. You not only have a well-trained, well-behaved, happy dog; you have a helper in your daily life. Because of all he does for you he deserves the best life you can give him for his whole life. This includes working with him, praising his appropriate behavior, taking good care of him, and keeping him on a routine. He is dependent on you for all his needs and in return he gives you love, companionship, and service.

You have TEAMWORK!

APPENDIX
Other Commands

EASY

Rather than a command, this is a warning; it's getting your dog's attention and redirecting his energy. Use whatever word or phrase that comes to your mind readily—"easy," "cool it," "careful." What you want it to mean is that he should stop whatever he's doing, settle down and look at you. It's not quite as much a correction as "uh-uh-uh," but it carries some of the same weight.

This is something that you will teach him over time. Using any of those words our voices automatically take on a tone of caution, and your dog will learn to recognize that tone. It will make him want to look to you for guidance on what to do next, and that's exactly what you're looking for. When you have his attention, even for a second, praise and if necessary give him a command he knows and obeys, like sit or down.

Start using one of those words any time your dog seems too excited or too bouncy. It helps keep him controlled in a variety of circumstances and makes training much easier.

UH-UH-UH

This is a correction, just like a jerk on the leash or yelling "No!" But it's much nicer for both you and your dog and much quieter when you're out in public. Just like "easy," it's something you will use over time, and your dog will come to understand its meaning. When you say "no," your tone automatically takes on a negative quality much like a growl and your dog recognizes that from his puppy conditioning. When you say "uh-uh-uh" your voice takes on the same tone but it's automatically softer, quieter, and more gentle. In the early stages of training you will need to tell your dog "no" frequently. Dogs, especially puppies, get into trouble and it's up to us to get them out. We have to give them lots of positives but occasionally we have to quickly and firmly correct when they are doing something wrong.

As you advance in your training and your dog is more tuned into you, your corrections come much less frequently and they shouldn't be as sharp or harsh. When you teach the complex skills contained in this book, your dog will often make a mistake simply because he doesn't yet understand all that's required of him. You need to let him know he's not doing it right but you don't want to make the experience negative. Try this phrase: "uh-uh-uh." Your dog will instinctively recognize the tone of your voice; he will know he's doing something wrong, but because your tone isn't harsh, he won't be afraid to try again.

TUCK THE TAIL

Sometimes you may find it helpful to have your dog pull his tail out of the way. A waitress in a restaurant with her hands full or a student with his nose in a book might not see your dog's tail sticking out from under the table.

It's not an easy command to teach because you can't hold a treat in front of the tail and have it follow your hand. Some dogs are always wagging their tails so they are always out and in motion. But you might want to try.

Sit your dog beside you and give him a stay command. Use your foot or your hand and gently push his tail into his body as you say "tuck your tail" or simply "tuck." Be quiet in the way you issue the command and also praise quietly so he doesn't try to wag his tail in response to your excited voice. Hold the tail against his body for a few seconds as you say "good tuck."

If you are unable to reach his tail with either your hand or your foot, you might be able to push on the tail with something like a long-handled reacher, or use a friend to help. As you give the command, your friend should kneel beside your dog and gently push the tail against your dog's hip and hold it there while you praise quietly. Your dog will automatically wag his tail from all this attention so you and your friend must both be patient and calm. Don't make your dog afraid of someone leaning over him.

You will have to practice faithfully over a long period of time for him to fully understand what this command means. He will have absolutely no idea what's going on at first. Many dogs never learn to obey this. But you might reach a point where you can position his tail and he will keep it there. Remember, however, that anything attracting his attention may result in a wagging tail and you'll have to position it all over again.

Most important, you need to become aware of the position of his tail, and any time it might be in the way you need to remedy the situation. You may need to have your dog move farther under the table or to the other side of you—whatever it takes to make him safe.

MOVE

It's very important for you to teach your dog to move out of your way. It's a safety issue for both of you. You don't want to trip over him nor do you want to run over him in your wheelchair. Many dogs seem to like to rest right in the way. They are bonded and like to be close to you. For some dogs it's a dominance trait. Whatever the reason, it's wonderful to have your dog close, but it's critical that he get out of your way without hesitation. Because you are the pack leader, it's natural for your dog to accept that he must move for you. Begin now to consistently demand that he move every time he is in your way.

The "move" command is easy to teach, and if you use it regularly your dog will begin to move automatically as you approach him. You can use any word or phrase you choose: "move," "beep beep," "excuse me." As always be sure the word you pick doesn't sound like any other command.

The easiest way to teach your dog to move is to say "move" and lightly touch him with your wheelchair, your crutch or your foot. Don't hit or kick him; it only needs to be a slight nudge that gets him to move. As soon as he gets up, praise "good move" and proceed forward. He will move out of your way and you can praise again. It takes very few repetitions to teach him that he will always be required to get out of your way. Soon he will be alert as you approach, prepared to move or respond to any other command you might give.

If your dog doesn't move on command, make sure his hearing is okay. If it seems to be a stubborn refusal to move, you need to reaffirm your position as pack leader. Give him the benefit of the doubt if he's sound asleep, but as soon as he becomes aware of you he should readily and happily move for you. Keep practicing this in conjunction with other areas that assert your leadership and control. (See chapter 2.)

SHAKE

"Shake" can mean shake hands which is a cute trick to teach your dog, or it can mean for him to shake his entire body. Teaching him to shake hands can usually be done in a few short sessions where you just lift his paw with your hand as you say a command such as "shake hands" or "give me five." Praise with enthusiasm as you shake his paw and give him a treat. Dogs enjoy this and your friends will be impressed. Be sure you don't allow him to paw you when he chooses. You can get hurt with those big paws and nails, and pawing can be a sign of dominance.

Teaching him to shake his body may actually be a useful service exercise. When your dog comes in from the yard, he may have all kinds of things in his coat. If you are on crutches, something as small as a blade of grass might cause your crutch to slip and you might really get hurt. If you teach him to shake on command before he comes into the house, anything on his coat will stay in the yard where it can't hurt you.

This isn't as easy to teach as shaking hands, but there are a couple of methods for you to try. Dogs shake regularly. If you say "shake" every time he does, your dog will come to associate the action with the words. Be aware of the word you choose for this exercise. "Shake" may sound too much like "take" and may be confusing to your dog.

It might take a long time for him to make the association, so you might want to create more frequent situations for him to shake. You can flick a little water on his face or his back, and if he shakes, give the command or signal. Be sure to give the command as he's shaking. Keep your voice upbeat and happy and follow with praise that includes the command word—"good shake."

Remember that when you're in a public place and your dog has been lying down for a while, it's natural for him to want to shake when he gets up. That's not a good time. Place your hand on his back and say "no shake" until you're outside where it's more appropriate.

PRESSURE

Your dog may be able to help you simply by standing or lying on some part of your body to help your muscles or joints. Mary taught her terrier mix, Lucky, to lie across her back while she was lying on her stomach on a water bed. Once he had learned the down command, she had a friend help her teach him the correct position. She used a multiple command at first: "down; crack my back." This taught him that the down, which he knew, was to be performed in a specific place. Eventually she just told him "crack my back" and he would lie across the small of her back which put just the right amount of heat and pressure to help realign her spine. Obviously, you must be careful that your dog doesn't do damage to you. Check with your doctor as to whether this might be something useful or dangerous.

Sandra taught her bouvier, Hoss, to step gently on her shoulder to help pop that joint. She first taught him to place one foot on a folded towel, using the command "shoulder." Remember that your dog doesn't know a towel from a shoulder or a hole in the wall. At first he was very confused so Sandra had to be patient and upbeat, praising every time he tentatively stepped on the towel.

When he learned to do this on command, she placed the towel in the right position on her shoulder, lay down on the floor and gave Hoss the command. He didn't want to do it at first because this called for him to step on the pack leader. Because he was used to the towel as a target, he finally put one paw on it and Sandra praised profusely. After several short and positive sessions Hoss would actually put weight on the towel which helped with Sandra's shoulder joint.

Again, be very careful that what you're asking your dog to do won't be harmful to you. But it may be that the combination of heat and weight will provide comfort and pain relief to some part of your body.

LEG UP

Dogs have a tendency to get the leash caught under a front leg. If it's difficult for you to bend over, you will have trouble getting the leash out. Your dog can learn to help.

Any time it happens, let the leash drop so it's against his foot or lower leg and then pull out, not up. The pressure will usually cause him to raise his foot and the leash can slip out. As he raises his foot, say "leg" or "foot" or "lift your leg"—some command to associate with the action.

Your dog may struggle, especially if the leash is caught under his armpit, and he won't be able to lift his foot up to help. Don't pull against him because the pressure on that upper joint will cause him to struggle more. Try to get him calm so the leash is not pulling against him. Then lower the leash so it's against his foot. Be sure you then pull the leash straight out. Remember to say your command as he lifts his foot and try to use it every time this happens. Eventually he will understand that when you say "leg" he should lift a front paw and you will be able to slip the leash out easily.

KISSES—NO KISSES

If you have a dog that licks you all the time, you might want to teach him to do it only on command. Some dogs show submission by licking around the mouth of the pack leader, but for some dogs it's a dominance issue. You might not mind being "kissed," but your friends might not feel the same. Also, when you are out in public, children, especially in strollers, are right at dog level. The child might find it amusing to be kissed or it might really scare him.

Any time your dog licks at your face, say "give me a kiss" or some similar word or phrase. Praise "good kiss;" then tell him "that's enough" or "no kiss" and push him away. Praise "good no kiss." With a dog who enjoys licking your face, the "no kiss" command is much more important and will take longer to teach. You will have to be firm and serious and not allow him to lick you once you tell him not to. If you practice diligently, he will learn to wait until you give him the command to kiss.

PERSONAL EXPERIENCE

Use this space to jot down notes on different skills you taught your dog or different ways you found that worked. It will be helpful when you train your next dog. If you have something you'd like to share with others, please contact us at TOP DOG Publishing.